Murder
On Lewis Road
And Other Stories Growing Up Northport

JOHN TERRY

outskirts press

Dedication

I dedicate this book in loving memory to my parents, Jack and Theresa Terry. They showered me with love and kindness and gave their seven children a warm, fun and loving home to grow up in. Until we are together again on the other side of the rainbow, your loving son.

Table of Contents

Preface

I CONSIDER MYSELF to be very fortunate to have been born and raised in the town of Northport, New York, during a time when thank God, there were no smart phones or internet. It was back when family, friends and neighbors interacted and spoke to one and other in meaningful ways.

Growing up and listening to old family stories of how the Terrys have been in Northport since the Cow Harbor days, have stayed with me to this day and have helped me with the writing of my memoir.

All my stories before you are true to the best of my knowledge, derived from my strong childhood memories and all the stories told to me by my elders. My stories are written from a 1960s, 1970s perspective and tone and lack todays political correctness. It is not my intention to offend any readers of my memoir, it simply is the way things were back then. Political correctness was never a consideration 50 years ago. I have changed many but not all, of the names of the people from my past that I have written about.

In the summer of 1965 Northport was a time-forgotten, seaside hamlet on the north shore of Long Island about 50 miles due east of New York City. The Vietnam War was starting to rage, drugs, rock music and the hippie movement were all in full swing. Northport however, was still a small quite village, seemingly insulated from the outside world where most families knew each other and many fathers either worked on the water or broke their backs at Steers Sand and Gravel.

It was a town where parents never thought twice about letting their young kids run wild for hours outside, playing together or fishing down at the town docks. It was a town where all the Main Street merchants knew you by your first name and you were taught at an early age that you could count on any of them to help you if you got yourself into a jam.

Northport was a wonderful, special world for a young boy to grow up in but as usual, life has a way of throwing you a few curveballs. One such curveball was the horrific murder that hit way too close to home. These are my stories of Murder on Lewis Road and Growing Up Northport.

Kings Park Psychiatric Hospital

CHAPTER 1

A Demented Mind

IT WAS A dark, cloud-filled day that only made Kings Park Mental Hospital look even more uninviting. My grandfather, Charles Scudder Terry, sat quietly staring down at the floor, as if he had dropped something but was unable to move to pick it up. He was waiting for my father to finish up a meeting with the hospital's chief psychiatrist. My dad was reviewing the doctor's results of my grandfather's in-house evaluation my father had arranged.

Sitting next to Pop, as we grandkids called him, was a big orderly in his late thirties, dressed in his white state hospital uniform. He had a small transistor radio tucked into his shirt pocket and was softly listening to the Yankee game being played that day. Mickey Mantle, the pride of the Bronx Bombers, who my father played a round a golf with the summer before, had just ripped a three run RBI against the visiting Red Sox, clutching another win for the Yanks. The orderly smiled at the thought of picking up his winnings from a local bookie he bet with from time to time. He turned to my grandfather and said, "Well Chuck, it looks like old Teddy boy here is going to have steak and chase some ladies tonight." My grandfather looked at Ted but said nothing, he simply returned his gaze back to the grey linoleum floor and re-entered his lost reality.

The door to the doctor's office opened and my father started to walk out but quickly turned and made it clear to the head shrink that he was making a terrible mistake. His father needed to be committed, not sent home.

My father, being the only one of his siblings able to take care of his elderly parents, knew in his gut that his father had major mental issues. Pop was constantly agitated, and often couldn't recognize his surroundings and loved ones which led to fits of anger before subsiding back into a peaceful nothingness. My father had to come up with some kind of a plan to address Pop's eroding mental health before he slipped further and further into a dark abyss.

CHAPTER 2

A Stroll Down Main Street

THE VILLAGE OF Northport and its harbor have a way of getting into your blood and never letting you go. Northport has a beautiful downtown along Main Street where you can still see the old trolley rails embedded in the concrete. Cars still park on an angle along Main Street as they did 100 years ago when Woodrow Wilson was our country's 28th President.

Main Street ends at the edge of Northport harbor, where the town docks and park are located. Northport harbor is considered by many to be one of the most picturesque harbors in New York State. In the '60s, Northport, due to its size and somewhat off-the-beaten-track location, hadn't attracted any of the larger national stores. Northport got its first supermarket, the A&P, around 1967, and McDonalds didn't plant its flag in town until 1972. This only added to the charm of Main Street and the Village. Back in July of 1968 it was truly a summer wonderland for my friends and me.

Although Main Street started up at five corners, to me, the true village started where Main Street intersected Church Street and Ocean Avenue. There's the Catholic church on one side and the Presbyterian church on the other. When I was a boy living on Seaview Avenue, we would get downtown by taking the path through the woods behind the Presbyterian church that emptied onto Main Street. Main Street was back then and is still today the epicenter of Northport, with many retail stores, shops, restaurants, pubs, the old library, a Chinese laundromat and our beloved one-screen movie theater.

The first storefront I would come upon was My Fair Lady, a very popular women's hair salon. It was here where my mother and Aunt Ella would get their hair done up on Saturday mornings. It was part of their getting ready ritual they performed each week, so they would look just right to go out to dinner with my dad and Uncle Bobby. On most Saturday nights that meant dinner down on the water at Mariner's. A lot of times I would put my fishing pole and bucket up against the building and walk in to the Lady, as my uncle often called it, to say hi to mom and Aunt Ella. They would both have their heads stuck inside these huge hair dryers, while reading lady magazines and chatting with other women who hoped their new hairdos would catch their husbands' eyes. I knew my Aunt Ella was always good for a nice crisp dollar bill, which meant I could stop by the Greek's (Northport Sweet Shop) for a cheeseburger and a black & white ice cream soda after a long morning of fishing and horsing around town with my friends.

My next stop on the way to the docks was a quick look into Jenelton's Linoleum store. I would always wave to Jelly Bean, Mr. Jenelton. Dad said he got that nickname when they were kids. If you looked sideways into Jelly Bean's storefront window you would see a very funny, distorted reflection of yourself. All the old-time local kids knew of this glass window reflection trick. Poor Jelly Bean always had a spray bottle of Windex and a rag close by, but he never gave us any trouble. That was Northport back then.

The next building I'd pass was the Northport movie theater. It was the same theater where my dad and uncles would go to see movies when they were my age. It had three sections of seats on the ground level and a great balcony. Some of my fondest memories occurred within the walls of that theater. I became a true movie junkie, spending countless hours on rainy and cold snowy days with my friends in the theater. I watched *Mary Poppins, Swiss Family Robinson*, most Disney movies, John Wayne double features and Clint Eastwood

Spaghetti Westerns. I can still remember as a young boy getting into a movie for 30 cents and purchasing a Coke and popcorn for 20 cents more. As young teenagers my friends and I would cause all sorts of trouble in the theater, just to be chased out by the older ushers.

I remember one time the theater was running a gory horror flick called *Mark of the Devil*. The theater handed out promotional barf bags, like the ones you find on some airplanes, to customers entering the lobby. My friends and I knew this beforehand and came to the theater with a few sandwich bags filled with creamed corn. Just at the right moment we threw the creamed corn over the balcony onto the unsuspecting moviegoers below, making them think they were just puked upon. We ran out of the theater that night. I stayed away for more than three months until all was forgotten. And I can't leave out my awkward attempts with a few girls in my class up in the dark, smoke-filled balcony. Man, I loved that theater.

Another funny observation was the fact that our good buddy, Jeremy Brinsmead, who had moved to Northport from England back in the 2nd grade, was one of the biggest culprits causing all sorts of trouble at the theater and two years after Mark of the Devil, Jeremy had landed himself a job at the theater as one of their ushers. I guess it takes a trouble maker to catch a trouble maker.

A few doors down Main Street was the police station where down in the basement was a special place for my friends and me: the PAL (Police Athletic League) club room. A kind retired man ran the place. Everyone called him Uncle Charlie even though he was not an uncle to any of us kids. Inside the club was a pool table, a wooden shuffle-board—the kind you see in old-time bars—and a baseball-themed pinball machine. The club was a place for kids, but only boys seemed to hang out there. I don't think I ever saw a girl in the PAL club room. There wasn't much for girls back then.

In the winters the PAL would take us to see roller derbies and even rodeos at the Long Island Arena. The arena people would put down on the floor a couple of feet of wood shavings and then let the fun be-gin. I watched in amazement as cowboys, who at the time I thought were the bravest men in the world, climb onto the backs these giant bulls with their huge horns ready to tear into anyone foolish enough to get in their way. Most times the cowboys would be quickly thrown off the bulls and the rodeo clowns would run out to distract the tormented beasts just long enough for the cowboys to make it to the safety of the fence. Pure excitement for a ten-year-old boy.

My favorite two things the PAL offered were the summer baseball outings to Yankee Stadium and the winter bowling league. For just a few bucks we would go by bus to see the Yankees play ball.

There was a list of games you could sign up for on Uncle Charlie's clipboard. The two most popular games of the summer were the games the Yankees gave away a ball and a baseball bat. That tradition didn't last much past the early seventies.

One time, a couple of my friends and I roamed around the huge stadium and ended up in the press box section, where all the sports reporters were plugging away at their Royal typewriters. It was the year that the Yankees' first baseman, Joe Pepitone, had injured his arm and he was hanging out up at the press box. We all yelled, "Joe, can you sign our programs?" He turned, looked at us, and told us to go fuck off. What a jerk. Later in life I learned that many sportswriters said Pepitone could have been a much better player, but he was more interested in trying to be like Mickey Mantle, partying and chasing women.

In the fall a very nice old man named Grandpa Newton ran the bowling league up at the Larkfield Lanes in East Northport, of which I was a member. He was the grandfather of a family, the Newtons, who lived up the street from us on Woodhull Place. My older sister, Theresa, was friends with Carol, one of their daughters, and our families went to the same church. Our league played every Saturday afternoon throughout the fall and winter months. I absolutely loved going bowling. I'm now 62 and I still bowl in a Monday night league. Thank you, Grandpa Newton and Uncle Charlie for all that you did.

One door down from the PAL was Northport Fire Station. Often, I would stop by to say hi to the Fire Chief, Mr. Berglund, who was also our close friend and next-door neighbor. Northport has a volunteer fire department like much of eastern Long Island. When the fire horn would go off, half the town's merchants would drop whatever they were doing, throw on their fire uniforms and race off to save their fellow Northporters. You'd be hard pressed to find a group of men with better qualities.

Mr. Berglund, Artie, was one of my favorite neighbors and family friend. He was a very warm, friendly man, built like a fire hydrant and he had an infectious laugh. He was handy with all sorts of tools. He captained his large Cabin Cruiser out of Huntington Yacht Club, raised rabbits, and, for years, he had convinced me, my younger sister Jean, and my brother Paul that there really was a Santa Claus. He dressed up as Santa every Christmas Eve and came to the back door of our house just before bedtime with bells ringing, belting out HO HO HO. He had me fooled -- that is, until one year, instead of falling asleep, I stayed up and I heard and saw Santa walk out of our back door. Not only was Santa now beardless, but he was also quite wobbly from one too many Jameson's my dad had poured him.

Another fond memory of Artie Berglund was the time a dog had treed a very large raccoon in an apple tree in the backyard of the Hotchkiss house. The dog was going crazy, trying to climb the tree and the raccoon was hissing its head off at the dog. Several neighbors and half my family went down to investigate. My mother, concerned that things were going to get much worse, told me to run and get Mr. Berglund. I ran like the wind and knocked on the Berglund's back door. Artie came to the door and after I caught my breath, I explained the situation. He didn't hesitate, he reacted has if he was Clark Kent, ready to save the day. Within seconds Artie Berglund burst out his back door like Superman, with his 12-gauge shotgun in one hand and my hand in the other, saying, "John, let's go get us a raccoon." I ran ahead of Mr. Berglund and yelled down at the large gathering of neighbors that they better hold on to their hats, Mr. Berglund was going to blow that raccoon to kingdom come.

Mr. Berglund quickly made all of us get way back. He loaded two shells into his shotgun and fired once, almost knocking that raccoon out of the tree, but still it held on. Again, Artie raised the shotgun up to his shoulder and pulled the second trigger. The echo of the gun blast went through our neighborhood and the smell of the gunpowder smoke filled our lungs. The raccoon was finished and fell through branches before hitting the ground with a dull thump. Everyone clapped and thanked Mr. Berglund for saving the day. I ran and got a shovel. I buried that raccoon under the big oak tree out by our garage. The dead raccoon was so large I had to dig a hole big enough for me to curl up in. Looking back, the treed raccoon episode reminds me of a scene out of the 1962 movie *To Kill a Mockingbird*, when Atticus Finch (Gregory Peck) had to shoot the rabid dog coming up their road.

My favorite all time thing as a young boy that took place each July in Northport, was the annual summer Fireman's Fair. It was held down in the Pit, as we locals referred to the homes in that area, which is now called North Bay Estates. As a matter of fact, there is a road down at North Bay Estates called Terry Road, named for my grandfather who worked at the now-closed Steers Sand and Gravel Company for many years and was one of their first employees.

On hot July summer nights, my parents would load us into the way-back of our station wagon and off we would go. It was a short ride up Ocean Avenue but with all our excitement and anticipation the ride felt as if it took forever. When my dad would take the left turn to head down Steers Avenue hill our hearts would start to race, the first sight of the lights and sounds and smells were intoxicating. We would stay for hours at the fair, going on every ride and playing dozens of games while eating corn on the cob, hot dogs, and cotton candy.

I remember one year in the late '60s word got out to the fair's organizers and the Northport police that a very large gang of Hell's Angels was planning on crashing the fair. The entire village was on edge. A dozen state police cruisers filled with huge troopers, patrolled the parking area and inside the fair as well. The Terrys, like many Northport families that night, did not go to the fair, fearing there was going to be big trouble. As it turned out, not one Hell's Angel rode into town. The talk around town the next day was that word got out to the motorcycle gang that they were not welcome, and so they decided not to tangle with the state police.

When I got older and went to the fair every night with my buddies our interest turned away from the rides and instead focused on meeting up with the girls we knew and drinking beer in the parking lot. Life was wonderful.

A short walk past the fire station on the other side of Main Street was a clothing store called Ingerman's. Back in the '60s, Ingerman's was a store the whole family could shop at and was way more convenient than taking the ride into Huntington to shop.

When you walked into Ingerman's you were hit with the distinctive aroma of new cloth and leather. It's a smell I will never forget. The women's and girl's department were in front and the men's and boy's department was up a ramp to the left. Located in the far back of the store was the shoe department where a small German immigrant named Boris was in charge of footwear sales.

Boris was a true master of his craft. He would whip out his ice-cold metal foot scale and before we realized it, Boris would have our feet measured and have several boxes of shoes laid out in front of us. He also knew mine and all my sibling's names and was quite fond of my older sister Theresa. Boris told me when I got older that Theresa reminded him of a young Fraulein he once dated in Dusseldorf. Such freckles, he said. Knowing my sister, she probably flirted with the old Kraut just for laughs.

A few doors down from Ingerman's was the Northport Five & Ten, a store unlike any other in Northport. You entered the store through the large double swinging doors and entered a world of endless selection. The Five & Ten had every small household item imaginable throughout its first floor, along with a large selection of small gifts and greeting cards. The best, though, was the toy department located on the upper floor.

Matchbox cars first hit the market in 1953. When I was a boy in the '60s, many of my friends and I collected Matchbox cars, which had really grown in popularity. When you climbed the stairs at the Five & Ten, the first toys you came upon were the Matchbox cars. The latest editions, like the '65 Ford Mustang, were displayed in a beautiful glass case. My oldest sister Peggy had a white Mustang with black leather interior.

I'm pretty sure that car was responsible for my sister landing her first boyfriend, some tennis-playing nerd from Oyster Bay named Biff. She soon realized however, Biff was more interested in revving the Mustang's engine than hers. She quickly dumped Biff like a sack of rotten potatoes. The rest of the Five & Ten's toy department was well supplied with all sorts of toys for both boys and girls.

A few doors down from the Five & Ten and across the street was Terry's Jewelry, owned and operated by my father's first cousin Jerry and his wife, Dot. Jerry and Dot were family and socialized routinely with my parents, as well as my uncle Bobby and aunt Ella Rose. Jerry and Dot attended all seven of our weddings and as a young boy I would stop in just to say hi.

When my kid sister Jean got married, Jerry approached me and asked if I had any desire to purchase the business from him. I would have loved buying the business from Jerry and keeping the family name running. I would have expanded the business to include a larger selection of more youthful jewelry to attract customers, keeping them from spending their money in Huntington. Unfortunately, I didn't take up my cousin's offer. Too bad, I would have loved being a Northport Village shop owner.

Continuing my stroll down Main Street I would come upon one of my favorite stores, Craft's Stationary. Craft's, or as we longtime residents referred to it, Barney's, sold just about every major newspaper from across the US and the most popular magazines of the day. Craft's also carried a large selection of cigarettes, cigars and pipe tobacco. Best of all was their large display case that contained penny candy. They offered dot candy on strips of paper, Mary Janes, cigar bubble gum, wax lips, candy cigarettes, golden nuggets, bubblegum in cloth sacks, and a huge selection of chocolates.

The store was owned and operated by two of the kindest people I had known growing up in Northport, Barney and May Craft. Barney and my dad grew up together in Northport and stayed friends for life. Sometime in the '80s, Barney sold the store to the Arndt family of Northport and he and May retired and moved permanently to their vacation home on a side of a mountain in Vermont. We visited them one fall weekend and rode on Barney's tractor, had campfires in the woods, and hunted groundhogs using Barney's .22 rifle. That weekend I fell in love with the state of Vermont and found myself later in life living in Burlington for a time.

Two doors down from Barney's next to the savings bank was Bowman's Sporting Goods, a young boy's retail playground. By today's standards, Bowman's wasn't a large store, but old man Bowman was a whiz at stuffing that place with every type of sporting good a person could ask for. I stopped at Bowman's every time I went fishing, for Mr. Bowman always had an excellent supply of fat juicy sandworms I used to catch flounders and sand sharks. You had to be careful cutting off the worm's head; they had these sharp fangs they hid in their mouths and unleashed them when provoked. Luckily for me and my friends, flounders and most other fish in Northport harbor were incapable of resisting sandworms.

Each spring I would clean out the cellar or our garage and my mother would give me money to buy a new baseball bat. I had two baseball mitts growing up in Northport given to me on my 11th and 15th birthdays, each purchased at Bowman's. I was really intrigued by their selection of hunting rifles, shotguns and pellet guns.

We lived up on 46 Seaview Avenue in a big old Victorian (the home was originally built for William B Codling, one of Suffolk County's largest land owners and first developer of Asharoken) and we had a large yard. Back in the sixties, families that owned dogs rarely if ever kept their dogs tied up, unless of course the dog was a known biter. Our yard wasn't fenced in and I think it was common

Terry Home, 46 Seaview Avenue

canine knowledge among all the neighborhood dogs that the Terry's side yard was a lovely place to take a dump. I can't tell you just how many times my father, while mowing the lawn, would step in a large deposit, causing him to curse as if he was still in the Army stationed in New Guinea, yelling at his men. One day after stepping on a fresh pile, he'd had enough. He phoned the Northport police station and explained to the Captain, his childhood friend, how all the dogs were dumping in our yard. He asked his advice as how to handle the situation. The Captain suggested my father go down to Bowman's and purchase a pellet rifle and to shoot any dog bold enough to enter our yard to leave their calling card. Let me tell you, up until the time I landed a 250lb Hammerhead shark off the coast of Miami when I was 12, shooting neighborhood dogs from the windows of our home was one of my biggest thrills.

I was to become my father's look-out, his fellow soldier. On weekend mornings it was my job to spot a dog entering our yard. When I spotted a dog heading our way, I would run to find my dad in the house. He would instruct me to head to the laundry room to fetch the rifle and pellets and meet him upstairs.

The second floor of our home offered us an unobstructed view of our entire yard. I must admit, looking back, I think my dad enjoyed our dog hunting more than I did. On most hunts he would hum to himself as he laid out the pellets onto the window sill and pumped the air rifle to its maximum load. We smiled as my father carefully loaded a pellet into the chamber. Dad would wait till the last second when the dog would just be starting its downward squat to pull the trigger. You could hear the pellet zoom through the cold, crisp morning air and the distinctive snap of the pellet hitting the unsuspecting mongrel square in the ass. My God, the howling cries that came from those dog's mouths was as loud as Northport's fire alarm.

Dogs with short fur, like boxers, felt the painful sting much more than their long-haired cousins. The pellets rarely entered their skin but it sure as hell gave those unlucky hounds enough hurt that they were never known to return. They found someone else's yard to dump in. If we were to shoot stray neighborhood dogs today, my dad would surely end up in the clink.

Across the street from Bowmen's is the Northport Sweet Shop, or, as the older locals called it, "The Greek's." There were no derogatory intentions by referring to The Sweet Shop as "The Greek's." On the contrary, everyone in Northport welcomed and grew to love the Panarites family and their fantastic ice cream and sandwiches. You must realize, the time was 1929 when George Panarites Sr. opened his Main Street shop and back then there were very few Greek families living around Northport. If today, you heard someone on Main Street say let's go have a bite down at the Greek's they would be more than likely older or from an old Northport family.

I couldn't tell you just how many times I have sat at the counter down at the Northport Sweet Shop, eating cheeseburgers and washing them down with their world-famous black and white sodas. During the summer months, my parents would load us in the station wagon after dinner and we would go down to the Sweet Shop and order ice cream cones or Italian ice served in white squeeze cups, and then we would go for a lazy ride down to Waterside Park or a ride around Huntington Bay.

I moved away from Northport 46 years ago, but I have been coming back each year since. Every time I pull into town, rain or shine, I go to the Greek's for a black & white. One sip and I am transported back to 1968, sitting on the stool looking out the front window without a care in the world, wondering if the fish were going to bite. I can tell you this with certainty, most New Englanders wouldn't know a good black & white if it crawled up their ass and bit them. It's a New York thing.

Across the street from the Sweet Shop was the infamous Skipper's Pub. Skipper's, on the corner of Main Street and Woodbine Ave., has been a Northport drinking and social institution for years. I've been told the name Skipper appeared on the storefront back in the early 1940s. The local Northport fishermen and workers from Steers Sand and Gravel were known to frequent the bar. My father told me he and a lot of young single guys from Northport would use Skipper's as a starting place before going out into Huntington and elsewhere. This all took place just before Pearl Harbor when they all were in their late teens and early twenties and unaware all their young lives were about to be changed forever.

When the Japanese dropped their bombs on Pearl Harbor, Skipper's became the gathering place in town for the soon-to-be enlisted boys, where they could blow off some steam and proclaim their desire to send the Japs back to the hell where thay had come from. My dad and uncles told me that after the war ended and our men began to come back home, Skipper's was the first place returning Northport boys, now men, would go right after spending time at home with family. It was a place where our local soldiers could go hang out and catch up with old friends, a safe place where the healing process could begin. I'm sure there were thousands of Skipper-type bars throughout the country where our returning heroes were welcomed.

By the time the '60s rolled around, Skipper's had gotten a little "long in the tooth." It had become a real seedy downtown bar where too many local people drank away their worries and paychecks. Sad to say, my father's older brother, my uncle Charlie, drank his liver away at the barstool he sat at seven days a week.

As a boy, I would walk past Skipper's on my way to the town docks to go fishing early in the mornings. On my walk back up Main Street, I would pass Skipper's where the sour smell of cheap booze and stale cigarettes would hit me and linger well past Barney's. On many occasions I would see my uncle Charlie's Ford LTD parked out front. Sometimes I would poke my head into the doorway and say hi to him and my aunt Cush. They'd be sitting at the bar.

Many times, on hot summer days, they would call for me to come in and I would sit at the bar and have a Coke and talk for a while. I enjoyed talking with my aunt and uncle, but I always felt a little strange being inside Skipper's. The three of us sat on the barstools close to the door while several small groups of sad, lonely people sat hunched over at tables in the dark, searching for their lost dreams in the bottom of a whiskey glass.

Even at age 12, I knew my uncle and aunt and their fellow drinkers were lost souls. Uncle Charlie, despite his drinking, was loved by all of us and was a wonderful Irish storyteller. I like to think I got my storytelling from him. My uncle Charlie Terry died the winter of 1976 from cirrhosis of the liver. He was 59.

About three years later, Skipper's was sold and went through a major transformation. It no longer poured its poison to the local regulars; they all had to move on to other juice joints to drink their money away. Skipper's was now a trendy restaurant and pub, shiny and new, catering to the well-heeled Northporters and to the many tourists who visited our beautiful village.

The last stop on my stroll down Main Street ends at the jewel in Northport's crown: Northport harbor and town park. Northport harbor and park are the focal point, the pride and joy of the village and all its residents, both old and new. The *New York Times* once did a story about Northport. It read: "There are few if any towns in the state of New York with a quainter and more picturesque harbor like that of Northport Village." I have never met anyone who disagreed.

The park was the place young families could bring their kids to play on the merry-go-round and swings. It is the place the town gathers each Memorial Day to remember our fallen heroes.

During summer nights we would bring blankets down to the park to sit and listen to weekly concerts led by the band director and music teacher, Frank Leonard, who lived across the street from my family. The park was the only place in town where I have ever witnessed a family spreading a loved one's ashes into the harbor and a few hours later a wedding party exchanging their wedding vows. The circle of life.

Our village park and harbor became a central part of my young life. There were very few kids I grew up with in Northport who have the same kind of family connection as I did to the waters off Northport village. I grew up listening to stories about what life was like back in Northport when my father, grandfather and my great grandfather earned a living working the harbor and spent Sundays with family and friends in the park.

Believe it or not, my father, as a boy, was paid five cents for every water rat he could kill down at the docks and park. My grandfather laid out lobster traps and clammed the northern end of the harbor around Duck Island and Sand City for years. Most impressive of all was my great grandfather, Skipper Bill Terry. He was born in Northport around the end of the Civil War. He went to sea early in his life and rose to become the Captain of a four-masted, wooden hull schooner that served as a cargo ship, he sailed up and down the East Coast. He later became one of the first Coast Guard men at the Eaton's Neck Coast Guard Station as their keeper of the light house. My father and uncle were both born down at Eaton's neck Station and spent their early days living in the housing the Guard provided.

These facts fell silent on a young boy. As a grown man I truly appreciate and acknowledge just how much the local waters have meant to my family. There have been many times over the last 45 years since moving to Boston that I have wished I had never left Northport and its harbor, both of which will forever hold me in their salty grip. Who knows what path I would have chosen if I had never moved from Northport? I like to think the path would have led me to the sea like my family before me.

My great-grandfather, "Skipper Bill" Terry, top left.
Courtesy of the Northport Historical Society.

CHAPTER 3

Captain Jack

DAD THANKED TED and slipped him a five-spot for watching Pop. He grabbed Pop by the arm and said, "Come on dad, I'm taking you home to Mom." On the short ride home, my grandfather stared out the window, a blank expression on his face, unable or unwilling to talk to my father. It was a look my father had seen before.

My dad was a Captain in the Army during WWII and was stationed in New Guinea and the Philippines. He was lucky compared to most men. Dad was not a combat soldier, instead he oversaw a major supply depot, commanded a southern unit of men and had 50-plus local Filipinos working for him. Because of this my father never fired his weapon the four years he was overseas except to shoot a large sleeping python his men came upon. The blank look on his father's face was the same look as the soldiers who came back from the front after weeks of combat fighting the relentless Japs.

He knew Pop wasn't well and was very concerned about dumping him off at home with his 80-year-old mother. The two of them were both senile and were having trouble caring for themselves. My grandmother rarely cooked full meals, instead they ate Kellogg's Corn Flakes and their hygiene began to decline. My grandfather spent untold hours out in his work shop, just sitting in his rocking chair, never touching a tool or starting a project. Something had to be done.

My father planned to call Bernie Smith, his childhood friend who was now our family attorney and a New York State Senator and ask Bernie to consider helping him get Pop committed permanently. He felt it was the best plan of action seeing that his dad was slowly losing his mind. He wondered how long it would take Bernie to cut through all the state's red tape?

My father felt quite alone with dealing with his elderly parents. His only sister Mary surely would have helped him, but she was 250 miles away in Andover, MA., raising her own young family and teaching first grade. His younger brother Bill, who we all loved, had a falling out with my grandparents a few years before and stopped going to see them, even though he lived a few doors down the street. Uncle Bill would live to regret his decision to cut ties with his mom and dad. And my uncle Charlie, who I got my superb use of profanity from, was a functioning alcoholic who could not be relied upon to help my father. So, my dad had to bear this cross all alone.

Just how my once proud, strong and fiercely independent grandfather got to this stage in his life still eludes explanation. Back in the 1960's the medical community knew even less than today's doctors do about mental illness.

When Dad pulled into his parent's driveway, his mother was sitting on the back porch waiting for them. She had probably been there for hours. She came down off the porch to help with Pop and my father pulled her aside. He said to her, "Mom, why don't you go pack a small bag and come stay with me, Theresa and the kids for a while? You know we have plenty of room for you. Dad isn't well, and I'm concerned you won't be able to handle him if he goes off."

"Oh, Jack," my grandmother said. "I couldn't possibly leave your father all alone, I won't hear of it."

Well, that was that. Dad knew better to argue with his mother. Her mind was made up.

CHAPTER 4

You Never Forget Your First Midget

ON A SWELTERING summer night in 1966, my uncle Bobby and aunt Ella had joined us for a dinner of steaks off the grill, corn on the cob, baked potatoes and fresh tossed salad. We all loved having Bobby and Ella over for dinner, they added so much humor and excitement to our family dinner table. Bobby was retelling the story of how he and my dad last Christmas, snuck onto the Steer's property and climbed up one of their beautiful pine trees and cut off the top seven feet for us to use has our Christmas tree. My mother said it was the most beautiful tree my father had ever purchased. She wasn't told at the time that our prized Christmas tree was acquired illegally, my father knew better. Had they gotten caught by Mr. Steers, my uncle Bobby would have been fired from his job down at the gravel works for sure.

While my three older sisters cleared the dishes and got dessert ready for us to enjoy out on our screened porch, I decided to go out front and play.

I burst out the front door, jumped the three steps and started playing on the ground with my Tonka Trucks. I made believe I was a bulldozer operator like my uncle Bobby, working down at Steers Sand and Gravel. I began to hear a familiar tune, a faint whistling coming from up Seaview Avenue. I got to my knees and peered over the evergreens trying to see who was whistling. I spotted a boy about my age, judging from his size, walking down Seaview towards our home.

I quickly recognized the tune to be "Camp Town Races" a song that Ms. Baldwin, my larger-than-life southern music teacher, had taught all of us just a few months before at Ocean Avenue Elementary.

I thought, just who the heck is this strange boy walking down my street, whistling my song? I was put off by this intruder acting like he owned the street. I walked out to the front sidewalk to confront this stranger and as he approached, I froze, suddenly realizing that this boy had a full-grown beard.

The midget walked right up to me and held out his tiny arm to shake my hand and said, "Hey little guy, what's your name?" My heart was pounding. All I wanted to do was run back into the house to the safety of my parents, but I was frozen stiff, unable to move. The midget tried his greeting again but this time I yelled out "Daddy!" and ran up the stairs, through the screened door and into my father's arms, crying. "Calm down," my father said, and I began to tell him about the strange little man outside.

My father Jack calmly walked outside to greet the stranger. After a few minutes of my dad talking to the midget he turned to me and told me to come out to meet our new friend. I slowly opened the door and ran to my father, hiding behind and wrapping my arms around Dad's legs. Dad knelt and introduced me to Mr. Winston Hitchcock. Mr. Hitchcock extended his little had for me to shake.

Very slowly I took his hand and stared in amazement at the little man, my own size with a beard. Mr. Hitchcock's warm smile and friendly manner quickly melted my fears away. Dad invited Mr. Hitchcock to join all of us out on the porch for coffee and dessert.

I sat cross legged on the floor between my father and my uncle Bobby, listening to every word Mr. Hitchcock spoke. As it turned out, Mr. Hitchcock was an actor whose troupe was performing a couple miles away from our house at the Red Barn Summer Theater on 25A. Not having a show that night, Mr. Hitchcock had decided to stretch his legs by going out for a long walk.

On that hot August night, sitting on our porch while lightning bugs flashed, and katydids sang their summer songs, we all sat for what seemed like hours listening to Mr. Hitchcock tell his stories. He had traveled all around the world performing for the royalty of Europe to the common folk of Australia. I learned that night that Mr. Hitchcock never let the fact that he was a midget stop him from doing great things and having glorious adventures, adventures most larger men could only dream of having. He was truly a remarkable human being and I felt lucky to have had him walk into my young life, whistling down our street.

Three months later, on a Sunday night just before Thanksgiving, I was lying on the carpeted floor in our TV room with my younger sister Jean and brother Paul. The three of us were enjoying ice cream sundaes that Mom had just made us. We were waiting for one of my favorite Sunday night shows, *Bonanza*, to come on. Shortly after the start of the show my eyes widened with excitement at what I saw on the TV screen. "Jean, Paul, look who's on *Bonanza*!" I said. I couldn't believe my eyes. I screamed as loud has I could. "Mom, Dad, come here as fast as you can, our midget is on *Bonanza*!" Both Mom and Dad came running from the kitchen into the TV room. Jack and Tess stared in amazement, speechless, at the sight of our new friend Mr. Hitchcock, portraying a leprechaun. Hoss Cartwright was chasing our little friend to no avail. All five of us were shouting at the TV set for Mr. Hitchcock to run so big Hoss wouldn't catch him. What a night we had.

The next day in school I stood in front of the entire class and told them all about our midget. The following spring, we received a postcard from Mr. Hitchcock. He was down in Argentina having another adventure. That was to be the last time we heard from Mr. Hitchcock. For many years after I would lay in bed at night and imagine all the adventures our friend surely was having.

CHAPTER 5

The New Neighbors

IN THE SPRING of 1969, a new family moved into one of the other Victorians two doors up from us on Seaview Avenue. I saw the large moving truck back into their driveway and told myself that I would go ride my bike up there right after lunch to see if this new family had any kids my age. I told my mother my plan and she told me that when she was getting her hair done down at My Fair Lady that morning, Mrs. Allen, a local realtor and town crier of local gossip, told her that she had just closed on that house. She sold it to an Italian family from Queens. Their last name was Ippolito, she told my mom, and said Mr. Ippolito was a great big tall man with dark hair and eyes. It seemed that Mrs. Allen wasn't too fond of Italian people and political correctness was not yet a term that figured into too many people's minds back in the 60's. Mrs. Allen also informed my mother that they had three boys. Mom said I should ride up there and say hi to the family.

I bolted out the back door and hopped onto my new bike. It was a black Schwinn three-speed English Racer I had just received for my 12th birthday the week before. I raced up the short distance to the new people's house and found the three brothers sitting on their front steps, the youngest playing with a paddleball and counting. I jumped off my bike, walked up to the boys. "Hi, I'm John Terry and I live in that white house two doors down."

The oldest brother, Tony said hi and introduced his two younger brothers to me. Vinny, the youngest, was my brother Paul's age and the middle brother was in my grade and his name was Carmine. As it turned out Carmine was a good six inches taller than me and about 50 pounds heavier. Back then I wasn't exactly a slim Jim myself, but this new kid was big and fat. I began to tell them about the neighbors on the street when one of the biggest men I had ever laid eyes on walked out the front door. Boy Mrs. Allen sure was right. It was Mr. Ippolito. He was wearing a white muscle shirt which I would learn later in life was called a wife beater shirt. He looked at me and said, "Who do we have here?" I told Mr. Ippolito that my name was John Terry and I lived down the street. He stuck out his massive hand, 100 times bigger than little Mr. Hitchcock's. He asked me a few questions about my family which I gladly answered. I then asked him, "Mr. Ippolito, why did you move to Northport?" Without missing a beat, he turned and said they left Queens to get away from all the niggers that were taking over the place. Northport back then was 99.9% white, so I didn't know too many people of color, but I knew the word nigger was not the kind of word you should throw around so freely.

Later that night my parents were getting ready to go out to dinner with my uncle Bobby and aunt Ella as they did most Saturday nights. They almost always went to the same waterfront restaurant in Northport Village, called Mariner's. My dad was helping my mom put on her necklace when I entered the room. I hadn't seen my father come home from playing golf up at Indian Hills Country Club, so he warmly greeted me and said, "Your mom tells me that you met the new people that moved in." I said I had and began to tell them about the Ippolito's. I told them about the three boys, Carmine my age and the giant, Mr. Ippolito. "I wonder why they moved to Northport," my father said as he slipped on his sport jacket.

"I know why," I said. "To get away from all the niggers."

My mother gasped. "John Jr.!"

My father sat down on the corner of the bed, held me by the arms and said, "John in this family we never use that word, it's a hurtful word that should never be used, do you understand?"

I nodded and explained that I was just telling him what Mr.

Ippolito had said. Dad said he wasn't mad at me, it was Mr. Ippolito who he was upset with and reminded me that in our family we say negro, never nigger. He stood up and told me to go out onto the front porch to keep a look-out for my oldest sister Peggy who had driven to get the pizzas we usually had from Salvatore's when mom and dad went out on Saturday nights. I walked out of my parent's room and headed down the front staircase and heard my father say to Mom, "It looks like we have a bunch of knucklehead newcomers living up the street."

Carmine Ippolito proved to be a bit on the spoiled side. We were both in 6th grade that spring and I tried being his friend, but we were just too different. He didn't even like walking down town to go fishing. What kid didn't like fishing? He was a real momma's boy. My uncle Charlie, my dad's older brother who was well known for his dislike towards anyone who wasn't Irish, told me that a lot of boys in an Italian family are spoiled mamma's boys who spent way too long attached to their mother's teat. I really didn't know what that expression meant at the time, but it sure sounded like Carmine Ippolito.

That first spring and summer after the Ippolito's moved in me and Carmine would lock horns on a weekly basis, testing each other's strength and courage. Even though I was smaller, I was far from being small and I was much stronger and way more coordinated than Carmine was. Things between us came to a real head the first week of the new school year in September. It would prove to be the last time me and lard ass would ever fight each other, let alone be friends.

CHAPTER 6

Dad's Family

MY DAD'S FAMILY has been living on Long Island for more than 250 years. His grandfather, Skipper Bill Terry was born in Northport around the end of the Civil War and was part of the first Coast Guard, stationed at the Eaton's Neck Coast Guard station in Northport. He was Keeper of the Lighthouse. Before the Guard, Skipper Bill was the Captain of a four masted schooner, that carried cargo up and down the east coast.

My grandfather was Charles Scudder Terry, born in Northport in 1887. He worked for years for the Steers Sand and Gravel Company as their Time Keeper. Both he and my great grandfather were quint-essential down easterners. They were frugal, hard working men, not quick to show love or affection towards family but they were both good providers.

During the Great Depression my grandfather supplemented his income by fishing, clamming and lobstering the north shore of the island. He also secretly off-loaded booze from Europe during Prohibition from boats out in the Sound. He later learned those boats and the booze stowed below deck had belonged to Joe Kennedy Sr. of Boston. Thanks to the sea, my grandfather's strong back and the soon to be Ambassador to Great Brittan, he could keep plenty of food on his family's table.

My father's mother was Loretta Nelligan born one town over from Northport called Centerport in 1895. She was one of five children from a devote Catholic family. My grandmother was the parent that dished out the love and affection to her children and was totally committed to my grandfather. She was, however, not what you would call a pretty woman; she was tall, thin and wore thick glasses and if I remember correctly, she had a bit of a hairy upper lip. A great mother nonetheless.

My father grew up with two brothers, one older by three years named Charlie, and one three years younger named Bill. Dad had a kid sister Mary, who we all adored, who was ten years younger than my dad.

CHAPTER 7

Mom's Family

MY MOM'S MOTHER'S family were Macwards from Scotland. Her Mom was one of six daughters who after migrating to the states in the early 1900's all the sisters graduated from Hunter College in NYC. This was very unheard of back in that time. Most young girls before WWI never went onto college. The sisters were quite modern in their thinking for their time and my great aunt Grace was very involved in the Women's Suffrage movement, protesting throughout the city and state for a women's right to vote.

My grandmother Theresa was a NYC school teacher. Her oldest sister Mary married and became a housewife and mother. Her other two older sisters, Margaret and Rosily, became Catholic Nuns and taught high school in a very expensive Catholic school on Park Avenue. Her sister Tan was a NYC Librarian and the youngest sister Grace, married well and became the free-spirited protester and great Aunt we loved to see.

My mom's dad, William Brady, was a hardworking, kind, Irish immigrant stone mason. My mother had one sibling, Bill, my uncle. They lived in the Bronx and bought a small summer bungalow in the Waterside Park section of Northport. Mom's dad passed away when she was two.

CHAPTER 8

Jack and Tess

MY DAD, JACK, was born in Northport in 1920. My mother was born in the Bronx in 1921. My father was a townie and my mother was a city girl who spent the summers in her bungalow at Waterside Park with her mom, older brother Bill and her spinster aunt Tan, the librarian.

Waterside Park, a section of Northport, was a small enclave of summer bungalows and had a beautiful private community beach at the bottom of the north shore cliffs that required stepping down about 200 wooden steps. The hard part was the long, hot climb back up.

There was also a beautiful wooden dock that shot out into the sound for about 100 feet. Waterside dock was an excellent spot for fishing and at high tide we kids could jump off the diving board and swim back to shore. If your folks allowed you to use the diving board, you knew you were getting older.

During high school my father worked as a soda jerk at Jones's Drug Store on Main street in the village of Northport. Mom would find any reason to go into Jones's so she could see dad. Mom and dad started dating and it didn't take long for them to fall in love over black and white ice cream sodas. They tied the knot shortly after my father joined the Army right after Pearl Harbor.

My dad for his time and surroundings was a very bright, well dressed, outgoing smooth talker who came back to Northport as a Captain after the war and quickly found his calling as a salesman in NYC.

Dad was a very easygoing, kind man who rarely raised his voice and never punished me with his hand or belt. My father brought back with him from the South Pacific after the war two diseases, malaria and alcoholism. My dad, if I were to guess, probably hit the bottle a little too much as a young man before the war. The war certainly didn't curtail my father's consumption. On the contrary, being 9,000 miles away from home in a war in the middle of the Pacific, along with his duties in the army, only made drinking that much easier for my father.

Dad was a Captain in a Quartermaster unit, overseeing a huge supply depot on the coast of the Philippines. It was a very important position, for without supplies the army was doomed to fail. As one can only imagine, my father was able to get his hands on all sorts of supplies from back home, including booze. And to make matters worse, most of the men under his command were from Kentucky.

Dad would love to tell the story of how one of his rebel sergeants came to his tent one day and asked permission for he and some of the other guys to go off into the jungle a ways and build themselves a still. It took my old man just ten seconds to tell the sergeant that he had his permission as long as my dad got his weekly cut. Dad used to tell us that the corn squeezing's those rednecks produced could peel the paint off a barn, but boy oh boy it sure as hell got them where they wanted to go.

After the war when dad returned home, he was greeted by my mother and my oldest brother, who was three. Mike was born a year after my father shipped out and was meeting him for the first time. After returning home my dad continued his drinking for a while until my mother gave him an ultimatum: quit drinking or she was taking Michael and leaving him. Believe me when I tell you, my mother would have done just that. So, my dad joined a newly formed organization called Alcoholics Anonymous. AA saved his marriage and life. My father stayed active in AA until the day he died in 2003. I never saw my father take a sip of booze, but I knew when he fell off the wagon, which happened a few times throughout my life. But dad always went straight back to the support of AA.

As a kid growing up in Northport there were a dozen times my father would bring home men down in their luck, trying to get the booze monkey off their backs, home for a good cooked meal. They were men of all means: doctors, businessmen, men who had only the clothes on their backs. They all shared one terrible thing in common, they all were alcoholics. My dad was lucky, he was able to keep his drinking in check, locked up in the vault has he would say.

He was a wonderful provider for our family. My mom and my six siblings never wanted for anything. When Dad passed away in 2003 many people came up to me at his wake and told me stories of how my father helped them to gain their lives back. Two people, a man and a woman, both told me that if it were not for my father's help, they probably would be dead. I don't know of too many people that have quietly helped as many people get off the bottle as my father did. To say I am proud of my father is an understatement.

He was so kind and loving towards me, showed me through example how to treat my mother and sisters and all women for that matter. He also saw in me sales ability and ushered me into his world of carpet sales, a world I thrived in and enjoyed for more than 25 years.

My mom was in many ways the opposite of my father. My mother was very shy and lacked self-confidence, thanks to a belittling overbearing aunt. But she was a very warm and loving mother who loved all seven of us equally. Besides having seven children, my mother also had eight miscarriages, which affected her deep to her core. It seems that every time my father got a promotion my mother would soon be pregnant. I think it's safe to say that dad was quite frisky and my poor mother, God rest her soul, was as fertile as a Jersey milking cow.

My mother, Tess, was kind, loving and enjoyed a good time out on the town with my dad and Bobby and Ella Rose, their dearest and closet friends. She was a very strong Catholic and the church played a big role in her and her family's lives. My mother taught me to be kind, loving and forgiving. And instilled in me my undying loyalty to my siblings. I can't tell you just how many times my younger sister Jean and brother Paul called out for my protection, resulting in me knocking the crap out of one of our many neighborhood kids.

CHAPTER 9

Dad's Friends

MY FATHER'S TWO best friends growing up in Northport were Jack (Footsie) Quinlan and Bobby (The Rose Bud) Rose. Footsie was a large Irishman with a heart to match his size. I even think the Quinlans and the Terrys were related one way or another. Footsie and my dad's friendship started very young due to our two families being so close. Footsie and my dad stayed friends their entire life but when they got older and started families, they saw less of each other. I think the main reason was because Footsie's wife, Tina, became sickly and needed Mr. Quinlan's complete attention. Footsie was a devoted, loving husband and father and was Tina's primary caregiver. This meant Footsie had to stay close to home. Later in life after Tina passed, Footsie became the Harbor Master down at the Northport Docks. It was a position he took immense pride in. And he had his hands full on busy summer weekends when there was an influx of out-of-town yuppie boaters seeking mooring space along Northport docks so they could spend their money at our local shops and restaurants. The last time I saw Footsie was Memorial Day 2005. He was in the lead convertible in Northport's famous Memorial Day Parade. He passed away not too long after.

My dad's closest friend was a man named Bobby Rose. Although he was not blood related to us, my siblings and I absolutely adored the man. We all grew up calling him Uncle Bobby. My uncle Bobby was closer to me than my actual blood uncles who I loved but my uncle Bobby was special. The Roses were an Italian family who lived on Ocean Avenue just a short walk from where where my father lived. Bobby lived with his parents, grandfather and two younger sisters. Bobby was a year behind my dad in school but were still the best of friends.

It's safe to say that both my father and Bobby considered themselves quite the ladies' men. My father was 5'11" and Bobby was only 5'5" but had an engaging smile and a sparkle in his eyes. Bobby had other attributes as well but unknown to most—not my father, however.

In the summer of 1939 after Uncle Bobby graduated from Northport High, he was betrothed to a local Northport girl named Jennie Coppola. Everyone in town new Uncle Bobby and Jennie were going to marry someday soon. Uncle Bobby had recently landed a job down at Steers Sand and Gravel. As it turns out, Uncle Bobby had a true knack for operating heavy equipment. His new job was just the ticket he needed to be able to afford to get married to Jennie. My father, on the other hand, was known around town as a young man that liked to play the field.

One Friday night in early July my father and Uncle Bobby were on a double date. Uncle Bobby was naturally with Jennie and my father at the time was dating Fanny Brett, the local newspaper editor's daughter. The joke of the day was Jack Terry was kissing Mrs. Brett's fanny.

It was about 11:30 and the four of them had just finished eating a late snack at Link's Log Cabin in Centerport. The guys had Coca-Colas which dad spiked with some rum from a flask he had in his back pocket. Jennie and Fanny both had strawberry milk shakes and shared a plate of French fries. They were driving the short trip back to Northport along 25A. Dad and Fanny in the front seat and Uncle Bobby and Jennie in the back. The windows down and Glenn Miller's new song, "In the Mood" was playing on the radio.

Bobby called to my dad up front to pull over, he needed to take a leak. So, my father pulled over and Uncle Bobby hopped out of the car and walked about 30 feet in front of the car and began to relieve himself.

Back in 1939 on eastern Long Island not every road or highway was laid out with street lights and this section of 25A was no exception. On this night in July it was quite overcast with no moonlight, so when dad pulled over and let Uncle Bobby get out it was so dark you couldn't see the hand in front of your face.

Dad could hear Uncle Bobby softly whistling to Glenn Miller's song and doing his business when he got a funny idea in his head. Without any warning, dad pulled the car head lights on and low and behold, right in front of them was Uncle Bobby, the Rosebud himself, in the flesh.

You might recall I mentioned a while back that my uncle Bobby, although very short for a guy, was blessed with some other attributes. As fate would have, the Rosebud was hung like a New Guinea Water Buffalo and I can bet you dollars to doughnuts that back in 1939 neither Jennie or Mrs. Brett's Fanny had ever seen a man's Johnson, let alone a real monster. My dad tells the story that when he flipped those car high beams on, the girls seeing Uncle Bobby with his Johnson in hand, they both in unison let out a gasp. Dad said Fanny Brett was so horrified at the sight of the Rosebud that she demanded that my father take her right home. Jennie on the other hand just smiled the whole ride home, thinking with delightful anticipation of her soon to be wedding night with Bobby Rose. When dad pulled up in front of the Brett's house Fanny turned to my dad and sternly said it wasn't necessary for him to walk her to the door, for she never wanted to see him again. That was the end of Mrs. Brett's Fanny.

CHAPTER **10**

Modell's

IN THE MID-1960S there was a retailer located in East Northport called Modell's. Modell's was a forerunner of Walmart. It was filled to the rafters with all sorts of products and departments that my little sister, brother and I explored freely, while our mother did the same. My mother could spend hours in the hardware department and felt safe letting us explore on our own. Modell's offered two things a young boy like me absolutely loved: a pet department and at the store entrance, a donut-making stand, which was home to the Baker's Dozen, 13 donuts. What 11-year-old could ask for more?

My mother came out of the house onto the back steps and called for me. I was playing with Jean and Paul in the far corner of our yard (we had the largest piece of property on Seaview Avenue, about two acres) and I came running to find out what my mom wanted. She told me to make sure the three of us didn't get too dirty because after she finished with the housework we were going to Modell's. Modell's. Just the mention of the word sent waves of joy through my body. Not only were we going to be able to check out any new animals that might be there, like an exotic South American bird or some fighting fish, but I also knew we were going home with a baker's dozen. I screamed with excitement, "Jean, Paul we're going to Modell's!"

I ran to my brother and sister and in our moment of excitement we stopped poking at the dead opossum we had found in the corner of the yard moments before, maggots still crawling all over it.

The three of us ran into the house where our mother made sure we washed our faces and hands. My mother said, "Remember kids, we're not shanty Irish; we're lace curtain Irish, and that means we never go out and about town all messed up."

Our mother would not have been pleased had she'd known her "lace Curtin" little ones just moments before, had finished playing one of our favorite games, dog doo on a stick. My little sister and brother absolutely loved it when I would chase them all around our yard with a hunk of dog doo on a stick. When you are 11, 8 and 5 it was sheer enjoyment.

She told us she would be ready in five minutes and for us to wait for her outside. Well, I learned very early in life that was family code for mom needs to use the bathroom, which meant it would be more like 20 minutes. My poor mother suffered from IBS her entire adult life. We would sit outside and quietly laugh at the funny fart sounds coming from the bathroom window. If she had known, we were laughing at her condition we would have never gone to Modell's.

We entered Modell's front lobby and pressed our faces up against the glass to get a good look at the automated donut-making machine. We smiled at each other as the donuts splashed into the hot oil. Our mom gathered us up and we walked into Modell's where my mom grabbed a shopping cart. She turned to the three of us and told us sternly, "You can go check out the toys and pets and I will catch up with you in the pet department; and remember, no trouble or we will leave the store without any donuts." No donuts? With that threat we had no intentions of causing any trouble. Unfortunately, trouble had a way of finding the three of us.

CHAPTER 11

The Spider Monkey

MOM WENT OFF to explore on her own and we three kids ran to our first stop, the plant department, where they had a walk-in green-house. We entered the hot room and our noses were immediately filled with the strange sweet aroma of exotic plants and flowers. We came upon a cool new plant that I read about in school.

"It's a Venus Flytrap," I told Jean and Paul. "It eats bugs. Let's find a bug and see if it will have it for lunch."

It wasn't long before Paul cried out, "John, I found an ant." I grabbed the ant with my thumb and pointer finger and mushed it a little but didn't kill it outright. We walked back over to the Venus Flytrap and I carefully dropped the half-dead ant into its spiny jaws. We looked in amazement as the plant closed itself around the struggling ant. I said, "That's one way to skin a chicken, let's go check out the pet department."

We ran to the pet department and we each took an aisle to explore. I picked the fish aisle, Jean went for the bird aisle, and Paul went straight for the snakes and lizards. I took my time, enjoying the large assortment of fish swimming in their tanks, then something caught my eye. Sitting on a table at the end of the aisle was the most amazing sight I had ever seen in Modell's. It was the Holy Grail of all pet store animals, a spider monkey. I was so excited I had trouble containing myself. I just stood there, staring at this monkey, calling for Jean and Paul to come running. When Jean and Paul saw for themselves just what I had discovered they too were overjoyed.

"What kind of monkey is it, John?" Jean asked. I explained to them it was a spider monkey from South America.

Our amazement started to fade while staring at the monkey, for all it did was quietly sit there staring back at us, as it if were a stuffed toy. Jean started to complain and ask why it was just sitting there. She grabbed me by the arm and said, "John, do something, make it move around."

So, with me standing there in front of the monkey cage, Jean on one side of me and Paul on the other, I looked to make sure that smelly, toothless old man of a store clerk wasn't spying on us. With no clerk in sight I grabbed the monkey's cage with both hands and began giving it a good shake, thinking this would really get him going. Well, get him going was an understatement. That spider monkey did the strangest thing I had ever seen an animal do. He was so mad at me for shaking his cage the way I did, the monkey reached down between his legs and grabbed onto his pink little pecker and at the same time it started to let out a God-awful screeching sound: EEE, EEE, EEE. Now the three of us were petrified at the sight of the monkey doing strange things to his pecker, or as my mother would call it, his GO GO. And then, from behind us: What on earth are you kids up to? It was Mom.

Our mother was a saint. Before meeting my father and falling in love, my mother lived a very sheltered life. She was raised by her widow mother (Mom's dad died when she was two) and her old spinster librarian aunt who was a closet alcoholic and belittled my mother often. My mother went to one of the most expensive, exclusive Catholic schools in New York City, Sacred Heart Academy. Margaret, her aunt, was superior of the community, and so she got to go there free.

Two of President Kennedy's sisters went to school there and they use to make fun of my mother because they knew she had no money. The Kennedy sister's bullying of my mother throughout high school I'm sure, was why we Irish Catholic Terrys were staunch Republicans, not Democrats. There was no way in hell my mother was going to vote for any dam Kennedy.

My mother had given serious thought to entering the nunnery like her two aunts, thank the heavens above she instead met my smooth-talking father and the rest is history. It was safe to say even after having seven kids she was still a bit prudish and very proper. Being confronted with this fowl monkey playing with his pink little GO GO was going to send her over the edge for sure.

"Kids, what are you looking at?" My heart stopped. At that moment I wished my father was there to deflect what was coming. "Hey, move away kids, so I can see," she said.

I stepped aside and my mother came face-to-face with our perverted spider monkey, shaking his Go Go at mom and screeching EEE, EEE. Mom was so totally surprised and revolted. It took her about 20 seconds to form words. I saw her grabbing the bar on the shopping carriage so tightly her hands started to turn a bright red, just like her face. When she was finally able to form words all she could say was, "That's disgusting."

Mom grabbed little Paul and threw him in the carriage and told me and Jean to hop on each side, something we would had never been allowed to do on our own. "I'm going to find that manager," Mom said, "and give him a piece of my mind." The manager was a tall man in his thirties and Mom found him on the loading dock, having a smoke with a young summer worker and stinky, toothless Charlie, the old clerk.

My mother, all 5 feet 1 inch of her, walked straight up to that young manager and proceeded to shake her finger at him and gave him a good Macaward tongue lashing. That poor big guy just stood there, shoulders hunched over, taking every bid of my mom's lashing and agreed to get rid of that disgusting monkey. Never, ever did Modell's bring in another monkey.

Mom turned that carriage around and went back into the store where she grabbed the three of us, still a little off balance from the whole experience and told us we were going home. She raced us out of the store so fast and all I could say was, "What about the baker's dozen?" I got a slap in the back of the head for that. When we got home my mother made us take a hot bath, even though it was summertime, just to make sure the filth of that disgusting creature came off us. I'm quite sure when dad got home from the city that night my mom took two valiums instead of one.

CHAPTER 12

The Rock

IT WAS LATE afternoon on a Sunday and once again me and Carmine were wrestling. My parents pulled over in the car to talk to me. They were driving my sister Theresa (Tede) to the airport. She was heading back to college up in Boston and my dad asked me if I wanted to come along for the ride. I said I didn't feel like going and my parents informed me that my sister Peggy was home to keep an eye on me, Jean and Paul and I was to go home in about an hour or when Peggy called me. I reached into the back seat and gave my sister a kiss goodbye and she grabbed my arm and pulled me closer and whispered into my ear, "Don't be too rough with momma's boy." We both smiled, and I waved goodbye. Tede stuck her red head and freckles' out the back-car window, yelling as my dad pulled off that we would see each other at Thanksgiving.

Me and Carmine picked up where we left off, wrestling and trying to knock each other down to the ground. Carmine suddenly released his hold on me and said he was sick of this. He suggested we have a real fight with punches and all but that we agreed not to punch in the face. I agreed but I had my fingers crossed behind my back. We faced off and began throwing blows into each other's body but for some unknown reason I just lost it. I threw three punches, one to the nose and two to each eye. Carmine fell backwards crying like a big baby and I was about to body slam him when out of nowhere his older brother Tony grabbed me and pinned my arms behind my back. Tony was a 10th grader and a lot stronger than me. Tony called out for Carmine to get up off the ground and punch the shit out of me. Carmine landed one punch to my forehead right before I used my leg to kick his brother in his shin as hard as I could. Tony yelped in pain and let go of his grip, giving me my opportunity to escape. I ran out of their yard and into the Robin's back yard. The Robins lived between our house and the Ippolito's. They were having a new septic tank installed and seeing that it was Sunday there were no workers around, just piles of sand and rocks. I stopped at the sand pile and turned to taunt the Ippolito brothers who were calling me every Irish slur I had ever heard. I started to call them a bunch of smelly Italian organ grinders, where's your monkey? When they began saying nasty things about my mother, I really lost it. I bent down and grabbed a beautiful three-inch rock.

I had the strongest throwing arm in my grade, no questions asked. I got a blue ribbon at our Ocean Avenue Field Day every year for the softball throw. While the Ippolito's continued to yell their Irish insults, I reached back with all my might and threw that rock as hard and as high as I possibly could. Looking back, I felt for sure that divine intervention kicked in. Lard ass never saw it coming. I on the other hand saw everything in slow motion. I watched with joy every rotation of my rock fly 100 feet in to the air high above the trees and come soaring down, hitting fatso Carmine Ippolito square in the head.

I think the entire neighborhood must have heard that rock hitting his noggin. It sounded like his head was hollow like a big fat watermelon. Carmine hit the ground hard. I had knocked him out cold and his brother fell to his knees next to Carmine, screaming for his father yelling, "John Terry had just killed Carmine!"

OH MY GOD, I had just killed Carmine Ippolito, I was going to be thrown into the back of the paddy wagon and sent up river. I ran as quick as I could up my back stairs into the house yelling and crying for my sister Peggy. She was in the TV room when I came in crying, trying to catch my breath. I quickly explained what I had just done, that I killed Carmine with a rock. Just then there was a terrible, earth shattering banging sound on our back door. It was big, hairy Mr. Ippolito yelling for me to come out. Peggy told me to stay put and went out onto our back steps to confront Mr. Ippolito. After much yelling from each of them, Peggy came back and said that I had to go out and talk to the crazy man. I slowly opened the screen door and found Mr. Ippolito standing on the sidewalk at the bottom of the steps. He was still taller than me and started to yell at me at the top of his lungs. I was so scared having this giant of a man yell at me, so for the third time that day I snapped. I began to yell back at Mr. Ippolito, calling him every name and swear word that I could muster. My sister just stood there with her mouth wide open. Even Mr. Ippolito was surprised at my foul-mouthed tirade.

I hadn't noticed, but our back neighbor, Mr. Berglund, had heard and saw all the commotion and decided to come to my aide. Mr. Berglund was a big strong Swedish man, Northport's Fire Chief and a dear friend of my parents and siblings. He told Mr. Ippolito very convincingly mind you, that if he didn't shut his mouth and leave our yard, he was going to dump him in Northport harbor. Mr. Ippolito said nothing, he just turned and walked back home. I ran into Mr. Berglund's arms, crying. I always loved that big Swede. Later that night when my parents returned from the airport, dad phoned Mr. Ippolito and the two of them agreed that me and Carmine were to give each other a wide berth. My uncle Charlie loved this story. The next three years in junior high we went our separate ways and never again locked horns. In 1980 I ran into Carmine down at the new and improved Skipper's. We were quite cordial that night knowing we had both matured since the 6th grade. Boys will be boys.

CHAPTER 13

My Two Aunts

WHEN I WAS a small boy living in Northport and well after moving to Andover, MA in 1973 at age 16, there were two women in my life that besides my own mother meant the world to me, my Aunt Ella Rose and Aunt Kathleen McArdle. They were not blood related to us Terry's, instead they were close family friends, unlike each other in most respects but both shared a mutual love for me and my family. The personal hardships these amazing women overcame would have broken most people. As a youth I failed to recognize and appreciate the obstacles and challenges they both had to overcome in life living in Northport. As an adult my admiration and respect for these two ladies was absolute. These are their stories of inner strength and character that has left an indelible mark on my life.

Aunt Kathleen

My aunt Kathleen was born in Ireland in 1900 as Kathleen Margaret Flynn, the youngest of eight siblings. Her mom died shortly after her birth. The doctor had warned her father that they should stop having kids after number 7 however, Kathleen's parents were devout Catholics and never considered any type of birth control.

Shortly after Kathleen's 13th birthday in the spring of 1913, her father came home and told the family that he was going to take his three youngest children and move to America. The four oldest children, all boys in their twenties, chose to stay behind in the home they had helped their father build, for all the Flynn men were fine carpenters. In July of 1913, Michael Flynn and his three youngest, Bridget 19, Peter 17 Kathleen at 13 walked onboard a ship and 8 days later they reached Ellis Island and New York, the state they would call home. Mike Flynn had a close cousin who was a brick layer who had moved a few years before and settled in Northport, landing a job with a home builder in Huntington. He wrote to Mike and assured him that with his carpenter skills he would have little trouble landing a job.

Mike's cousin was right, he did get hired by a local cabinetmaker that catered to the high-end home builders on the Island. Kathleen's brother Peter found work helping different fishermen for several years before enlisting in the Navy just before WW I. Kathleen went to school when she arrived in the states and became the first person in her family to graduate from high school. Kathleen came from a small country town in Ireland and moved to the small country town of Northport where she was perfectly content finding employment in town.

My aunt Kathleen was a wonderful cook and man could she keep a household clean and well fed. Word of her domestic attributes reached the Steers family not too long after Steers Sand and Gravel set up shop in Northport in 1923. The Steers family hired Kathleen as their new cook and house keeper, a position she took great pride in. The Steers family adored Kathleen and why wouldn't they? She was a bright, blued eyed young woman in her late twenties who was always cheerful and eager to please. And word has it, old man Steers couldn't resist Kathleen's baking abilities, especially her pies.

A few years later Kathleen met and started dating another Irishman in town named Jimmy McArdle. Jimmy worked for Steers Sand and Gravel as did many men from Northport back then. Jimmy was a kind man, no more than 5'2", but not sharpest tool in the shed, mind you. He and my aunt Kathleen tied the knot sometime around 1930 and purchased a small home on Highland Avenue in Northport, directly behind my father's home which was on Lewis road. Around 1937

Kathleen gave birth to a daughter and Jimmy insisted they name her Kathleen. Little Kathleen, has we Terry kids would later refer to her as, was unlike most children, she was mentally challenged. My mother told us growing up that Little Kathleen was on the same level intellectually as 9-year-old. She couldn't read or write and never went to any type of school, but you could have simple conversations with her. That's what it was like back then. Had she been born in today's world, Little Kathleen I'm sure, would have been mainstreamed at public school and taught how to lead a more independent life.

After Little Kathleen's birth, Jimmy began what was to become a lifelong problem with liquor. There was no question, Jimmy McArdle grew to become a functioning alcoholic. He continued to be a solid worker for Steers but began to spend too much time down at Skippers. My dad told me that back in the late thirties when he and his friends would hang out at Skippers it wasn't unusual for Jimmy to tie a snoot full on and then try to fight people. Jimmy, it seemed had the short man's curse as well. There were many times my father would load Jimmy into his car and drop him off in front of his home, only to return to Skippers to find Jimmy on a bar stool. Jimmy would run down the hill through the woods and would somehow beat my father back to the pub. He was never mean or violent to either of his Kathleen's, but his drinking behavior never changed. My poor aunt endured a life of social self-exile of not attending a lot of family and friends gathering and special occasions such as weddings, due to Jimmy's behavior while drinking. This is the way it would be until Jimmy's death in the late 70's.

My aunt Kathleen became close friends to my father's parents and he and his brother and sister loved her to death. When my father married my mother shortly after Pearl Harbor and left her pregnant to go off to war in the Pacific; it was our aunt Kathleen who befriended my mom and helped her set up home. And Kathleen was invaluable to my mother after my older brother was born in 1942. My mother was a city girl from the Bronx that spent summers in Northport down at Waterside Park, a beach section of Northport. Being an outsider, she had very few girlfriends at the time, so mom and Kathleen developed a lifelong friendship. Kathleen helped my mother after returning from the hospital with all seven of us and she was there for a shoulder to cry on through the eight miscarriages my mother had.

My aunt Kathleen was always a part of my life. I can't remember never remembering her in my life. By the time me, my younger sister Jean and brother Paul were little in the late 60's aunt Kathleen had stopped working for the Steers family. We lived in a big house on Seaview Avenue and my mother would pay aunt Kathleen to come once a week to clean the house and little Kathleen would do ironing for my mom. And let me tell you, little Kathleen could press a shirt and pair of work pants for my father better than the Chinamen down at the laundromat on Main Street. Our oldest sister Peggy likes to think she is the best ironer of all time, but she couldn't hold a candle to little Kathleen.

With 7 kids and a husband you can imagine all the house work it took to make things run smoothly. My mother could have handled it all on her own, but she and Dad helped aunt Kathleen giving her a little extra speeding money each week. But that's not to say my mother didn't enjoy a once a week break where she could go off each week for several hours doing food shopping and other errands.

The two Kathleen's usually came each Friday when we were in school. That meant every Friday I would burst into the kitchen after Ocean Avenue would get out to find my mom and Aunt Kathleen having a cup of tea and over on the kitchen counter there was always a freshly baked pie, cake, brownies or cookies waiting for me and my sister and brother. And just for the record, everything that women ever baked was from scratch. It would have been a cold day in hell before my aunt Kathleen would ever make a dessert that came out of a box of Dunkin Hines.

Besides cleaning our home for my folks, aunt Kathleen would come stay with us when my parents would go away often on pleasure trips and my father's business outings. This was happening when me, Jean and Paul were the only kids in the house. Our three older sisters were away at college and our oldest brother Mike was a Cobra Gunship Piolet fighting in Vietnam. It was these babysitting stays of aunt Kathleen where she really showed me just how much she loved us and how much mischief she allowed us to get into when mom and dad were away.

My parents traveled like this during the late 60's and up to the time we moved away from Northport in 1973. By this time however, aunt Kathleen suffered from a very bad case of osteoporosis which left her vey hunched over so much so she had to sleep sitting up in one of our living room chairs. Even with this condition she still managed to take care of the three of us. With her hairnet in place, cigarette under her top lip with a huge ash hanging from it she would get us ready for school, clean the house and always have a fantastic meal for us after a day at school. When we came in from school, she would always be at the kitchen table drinking hot tea. She used those cans of Carnation sweet condensed milk to cream her tea. I often would sit and talk to her about Ireland and ask her to speak in Gaelic and ask her what Northport was like back when she came to the US. Aunt Kathleen would say two things to me most times at the kitchen table. With her still thick Irish brogue she would say to me, "I, Johnny, now promise your aunt Kathleen that you'll marry a fine Irish Catholic girl." Then she would ask me what I wanted for dessert, an apple pie or "one of me chocolate cakes."

Like most young kids, we got into trouble. We loved it when Aunt Kathleen would come babysit us when our parents were away. A few times we played practical jokes on the old gal which the three of us thought were hilarious but at the time I think for sure Aunt Kathleen failed to see the humor.

There was time our parents were going to Miami with Uncle Bobby and Aunt Ella. So naturally, Aunt Kathleen was coming to stay with us that week. Me, Jean and Paul took the tape recorder my dad had won in a business golf outing and went out on our front porch and started recording sounds of heavy footsteps, shaking of the windows and me with my deepest voice yelling to let me in. Our hope was to sound like some guy trying to break in. I hid the recorder behind aunt Kathleen's favorite stuffed chair she would sleep in. I tied fishing line around the on off switch and laid the line along the wall and up the stairs to our bedrooms. As usual, Aunt Kathleen was in the chair and a sleep by 9:30 thanks to a little Jameson dad always left for her nighttime enjoyment. At 10:00 the three of us crept to the top of the front stairs, we looked down and Aunt Kathleen was sound asleep, quietly snoring. For a moment I thought I wouldn't pull the fishing line, but the bad John was whispering in my ear to pull it, so I did. There was a short delay and I thought maybe something went wrong but then the recorder began to blast our recorded break-in.

Poor Aunt Kathleen, she awoke so quickly her dentures almost popped out of her mouth. Our golden retriever, Missy, was barking her head off. She grabbed both arms of the chair and began yelling in that Irish brogue, "Ay, wake up kids, Jesus, Mary, and Joseph there's a bloody burglar on the front porch trying to break in the house." She got up from the chair and went to the window, saw there was no one there turned around and found the tape recorder.

The jig was up. We couldn't contain our laughter for another second. We came running down stairs still laughing, telling Aunt Kathleen that we loved her and asked her to please forgive us. "You almost gave me a heart attack you silly kids, I'm too old to be having tricks like that pulled on me." She asked me to never do that to her again. Of course, I agreed.

When our parents arrived home several days later, they asked how we had behaved. Aunt Kathleen gave me a quick wink and said, "They were all angels, Theresa, we had a ton of fun." Aunt Kathleen never told on us all the years and pranks we hit her with.

The struggles she had to contend with daily, dealing with an alcoholic husband and a grown, mentally challenged adult daughter along with her failing health would have put most people over the edge. Instead, my aunt Kathleen McArdle never complained, held her head high with dignity and pressed on. Kathleen McArdle passed away in the late 80's. She will always be loved and remembered by me and all my siblings. My youngest daughter was named Meghan Kathleen Terry, in her memory.

Aunt Ella Rose

My aunt Ella was truly a remarkable woman. She wasn't a doctor or some successful business woman, a famous actress or not even a local school teacher. However, Ella Rose was one of the strongest ladies I have ever had the pleasure knowing. She possessed more internal strength than most and a kind loving heart to match once you got passed her rough and gruff exterior. Ella was quite the character and was known by most in Northport. She was the head lunch lady up at Ocean Avenue Elementary, where she ruled her kitchen with an iron spoon. I can still remember our gym teacher from Ocean Avenue, Mr. Marshall, walking through aunt Ella's kitchen and grabbing a cookie or some other snack. He knew all too well the heavy cost he would pay if Ella ever caught him with his hands in the cookie jar. I'm getting ahead of myself. Let's start from the beginning.

Ella Rose was born in the early 1920's as Ella Sedlack, into a dirt poor, dysfunctional family from Gary Indiana. Ella's father who had trouble finding work during the Depression was unable to keep things together. He turned his back on Ella and her family by crawling into a whiskey bottle. Shortly after Ella's 8th grade school year got out for summer break, Ella, while sitting in her back yard heard a gunshot. Ella ran into the shack of a house they called home and found her father hunched over in a stuffed chair with his brains blown out.

After Ella's father's tragic suicide, Ella never went back to school, instead she found work to help her mother with her siblings and hung on to her very bleak existence. I've found it necessary to tell you about my aunt Ella's sad start in life. I feel it puts things into perspective just how Ella got her courage and self-reliance, valuable qualities that she would call upon later in her life.

It was late spring, 1941, and my dad's best friend, Bobby Rose, like most able-bodied young men, had enlisted into the Navy right after the Japanese bombed Pearl Harbor on the morning of December

7th, 1941. Bobby was assigned to the Navy's Seabees, the Naval Construction Force. Bobby was an expert heavy equipment operator; he could pick up an Indian-head nickel with the blade of a bulldozer. He was first stationed at a Naval base out near Lake Michigan for his training before being shipped overseas. Bobby left back home in Northport his parents, two sisters and a lovely young local girl named Jennie Coppola who he had dated in high school and was now betrothed to. Bobby and Jennie planned on getting married as soon as we won the war. Keep in mind it was 1941 and society and social norms were way more conservative compared to present day.

Ella had gotten a waitress job in a restaurant and bar popular with the service men in the area, not too far from the base where Bobby Rose was stationed. Bobby and his running mates became regulars at the joint where Ella worked. It wasn't too long before Bobby and Ella became friends. Bobby was a short man, maybe 5'5" but he had sparkling blue eyes and a warm smile that could melt a girl's heart. Ella Sedlack was about 5'10" with brown hair and eyes, not fat but large boned. Ella was not what you would call a knock-out, but she was attractive nonetheless.

What happens next is as old as time itself. Two young people lonely, away from home, one looking at a long horrifying war and the other one barely scratching out a life in a Midwest Podunk of a town. One thing led to another and low and behold, Bobby Rose and Ella Sedlack had gotten pregnant. Bobby Rose, the upstanding young man he was, raised in a fine Italian Catholic family from Northport, New York did what he had to do. A few short weeks after and just before shipping out to the war, Bobby Rose and Ella Sedlack got married by a Justice of the Peace (no priest back in 1941 would have married them in a church) and Bobby made arrangements for Ella to go immediately by train to Northport and live with Bobby's family and have the baby, while waiting for Bobby to return home from the war.

It's 1942 for God's sake. Ella had never traveled more than 50 miles from where she was born. I can't even begin to imagine the courage it took for aunt Ella to step off the train at East Northport station, pregnant, holding all her worldly possessions in one small suitcase, and being greeted by her new father in-law, Frank Rose, Bobby's father.

Can you imagine what it was like for Bobby's mother and sisters to have been told the news that Bobby wasn't going to be marrying Jennie Coppola? "Why not?" his sisters would ask his parents. "He can't, your brother met a woman out west, got her pregnant with his child and now his new bride is going to live with us and have the baby here." It had to have left his sisters and mother speechless, gasping for air and explanations.

The shockwaves of this news must have spread like wildfire through a small town like Northport. Bobby and Jennie were a well-liked young couple in Northport and many people were looking forward to their union. And what about poor Jennie? Can you imagine what it must have been like for Mr. Rose to go over to the Coppola's home and inform Jennie and her parents that there would be no wedding between Bobby and Jennie and then explain to them the reason why? My God, you can't make this stuff up. A lot of people's lives were changed the day Ella Rose stepped off that train. A lot of resentment was soon to follow but Ella would rise above it all.

It was hard to send your only son to war. And it was no easy task to accept with open arms the strange young woman, pregnant and married to their son, now living with them under their roof. The Rose family had little choice, but they were good, kind people so after the initial shock wore off, the family helped Ella try to settle in and get comfortable with her new family and town. But it wasn't easy for either Bobby's family or aunt Ella.

My parents told me that Ella didn't have it easy being pregnant, living in a small village like Northport where she stuck out like a sore thumb. When Ella walked down town to shop, she endured more than a few nasty remarks, mainly from the younger women her own age that were friends with Bobby's former girlfriend. Ella held her head high and tried not to let the ignorant towns people's blinded view of her pull her down. What helped her most to get through the following years of Bobby's absence was the thought of the small baby she would soon bring into the world and Bobby's safe return from the war. She was hopeful once Bobby returned and they settled into their own home with their new baby, that just maybe, the remarks and dagger filled stares would stop.

Ella gave birth to a healthy baby boy that she and Bobby named Frank, after Bobby's father. Life in Northport for Ella began to improve after the arrival of little Frank. The looks and whispers behind her back became a thing of the past. The war in Europe had turned for the better for America and its allies. Hitler and his war machine were on the defense and the public was told it was only a matter of time before the allied forces prevailed. Ella didn't know it at the time, but she was soon to meet the woman that would become her closest friend and lifelong supporter; a woman who could relate to Ella's treatment for being an outsider living in Northport, my mother, Theresa Terry.

When Bobby and my father returned from the war, life got much better and easier for aunt Ella. Bobby got right back to work down at Steers and my dad started his career as a salesman, working for the large carpet mills down south. Ella would soon become the beloved lunch lady up at Ocean Avenue School. Thousands of Northport kids went through Aunt Ella's kitchen. She made sure every boy and girl at Ocean Avenue was well fed, even if it meant paying for the kid's meal out of her own pocket, which my mother told me she did countless times. Mrs. Rose never forgot where she had come from and what it felt like to go to bed with nothing in your stomach.

My parents and Bobby and Ella started a lifelong, inseparable friendship, traveling to Miami together many times and their weekly dinners down at Mariner's Inn. They became as much a part of mine and my siblings lives as any of our blood relatives. You can't pick your family, but you can pick your friends. Ella outlived both my parents and uncle Bobby. Aunt Ella Rose passed away on November 26, 2008.

CHAPTER 14

Murder on Lewis Road

THE ONLY ONE up early that August morning was my little sister Jean, who was walking back to her room from using the bathroom, when the phone in the hallway rang. Jean answered the phone and said, "Oh hi Pop, yes, my daddy's home." Jean walked into my parent's room and woke my dad and told him Pop was on the phone. My father's heart began to race. His father never called the house. It was always his mother who called. He immediately knew something was wrong. He grabbed the phone and said, "Pop you ok?"

"Jack, you need to come up here, there's something wrong with your mom." "Is she sick, did she fall?" The phone went dead.

My dad threw on clothes and burst through the back door of our home, scaring off a bunch of mourning doves in all directions. He took off in his car, raced down Church Street and screamed past Father Caton, who was sweeping the front steps of St. Phillip's and in less than three minutes screeched to a stop in front of his parents' Lewis Road home. He hopped out of the car and jumped the front steps, tripping, he caught himself just before slamming head first into the screen door. His hands were shaking so badly he had trouble getting the key into the door lock. He opened the door and walked into the front hallway, trying to adjust his eyes to the sudden darkness. He found Pop sitting in his overstuffed chair in his pajamas, just staring out into space.

"Dad, where's Mom? "my father asked. No reply, just silence.

My grandparent's bedroom was located right off the living room, it's door slightly opened. My father very slowly entered their bedroom, fearing for what he might find. The room was dark as pitch, the only sound coming from an old wind-up alarm clock that sat on the night stand. There was a strange odor of wet copper pennies in the air. My father took a small step into the bedroom and quietly called for his mom but received no response. He walked further into the room and stepped onto something wet; he froze, unable to take another step he began to hyper ventilate. He looked down, and in the dimly lit room, lying face down in a pool of blood was his poor, sweet mother, her head split wide open, his father's ball peen hammer lying in the blood-soaked rug next to her slain body.

He knew instantly his mother was dead. Tears began to roll down my father's face. He turned, ran to the bathroom and puked in the toilet. Shaking uncontrollably, he pulled himself up to the sink and splashed water onto his face to try to gain some composure. My dad caught a glimpse of himself in the small bathroom mirror. He was white as a ghost with tear filled, swollen eyes. For a second time he splashed cold water onto his face. He walked back into the living room where Pop was still sitting, staring into space. Dad walked over to him, placed a hand on his shoulder and quietly whispered, "Oh my God, Dad, what did you do?"

He led my grandfather to the kitchen table. He grabbed the phone and called the Northport police. "This is Jack Terry, I'm up at my parent's house on Lewis Road, I just found my mother, dead on the bedroom floor."

My grandparent's home was only a mile away from the police station. It took the first cop car only two minutes to get to my grandparent's home. An ambulance arrived right behind the police, followed by a young reporter from the *Northport Journal*. A carload of the town's top brass from the police squad soon arrived. The reporter was told by one of the cops to back off, show some respect. My dad knew most of the cops on the Northport Police, having grown up with the Captain and Chief. Percy Ingerman, who lived a few blocks down, arrived and quickly took my father to the side. Percy was the partner of Ingerman and Smith, our family's attorneys who had an office on Main street in Northport. He told my father, "Make sure that your father doesn't say a word." Dad told him that wouldn't be a problem since he hadn't spoken in weeks. Captain Sweeny led my grandfather out of the house and placed him in a squad car and told my father they would go easy on him. Percy followed the car to the station to be with my grandfather.

Neighbors began to gather out front on the street, milling around and whispering. My dad's younger brother, my uncle Bill, pushed passed the neighbors and found my dad in the kitchen. "What are we going to do, Jack?" my uncle asked.

"What can we do, Bill? We need to arrange for Pete Nolan to come get Mom and go down to the station and make sure they don't crucify dad."

News of the Terry murder went through Northport like oats through a cow, it was all anyone in town could talk about, people were in shock. My grandmother's murder was only the second murder to have taken place in the village of Northport, since the town changed its name from Cow Harbor to Northport in 1837. We Terrys were one of the older families in Northport. There was Terry Road down in the Pit, named after my grandfather no less, Terry's Jewelry store on Main Street, owned by my dad's first cousin, Jerry Terry, and Lewisy Fuel and Oil was owned by our uncle and aunt, George and Jen Lewisy and their two sons, Buddy and Dick, my second cousins. Our aunt Jen was my grandmother's sister. Most people in our small town knew us or knew who we were.

News of my grandmother's gruesome murder was splashed upon the front page of the *Northport Journal* and Long Island's *News Day*. Several radio stations also reported on the horrific family murder in the sleepy seaside village of Northport. There was no escaping the staring eyes and the small-town gossip that followed.

Percy Ingerman and his partner, Bernie Smith, arranged for Pop to immediately be taken back to Kings Park Mental Hospital instead of going to jail. Bernie would later go before a judge to have my grandfather committed permanently where he would live out the rest of his tormented life.

CHAPTER 15

Eyes of Contempt

NOLAN'S FUNERAL HOME was the first choice for most Catholic families in Northport and the surrounding towns to have their deceased loved one "laid-out." Pete Nolan Jr. was in his early thirties and was starting to take over the family business from his father. He greeted our family with utmost respect and understanding when we arrived, the Nolan's had known my family for years and due to the size of my family we were long steady customers.

It was one of the largest wakes Northport had seen in years, with long lines running up Larkfield Road. I heard my uncle Charlie, as did most people standing in the large lobby, complain to my dad that there were so many people here he didn't even know. "A lot of them sons of bitches," Uncle Charlie said, "are just strangers wanting to see the women who got her head bashed in by her deranged husband." Peter Nolan heard uncle Charlie's rant and quickly led him down the stairs to his office where there were a few other family friends and relatives throwing back shots of Jameson. A real Irish funeral mind you. Uncle Charlie gladly took his place in line and started back up with his ranting but at least he was out of ear shot from the people upstairs paying their respects to my family.

Visiting hours were held both in the afternoon and evening. My poor father and his siblings stood for hours greeting and accepting warm condolences from hundreds of towns people. Half the police force, every Priest and Nun from St Phillips, most of the firemen and just about everyone who worked at Steers Sand Gravel, including Mr. Steers himself, attended grandmother's wake.

It's one thing to have a wake for your mother after her passing from natural causes; I can assure you it is a total foreign experience to hold a wake for your mom as a result from her having been brutally murdered by your insane father. What an ordeal. How was my father ever going to be the same after dealing with this unimaginable experience? Only time would tell.

My grandmother was buried the following day on Saturday. We were told by my mother that we didn't have to go to church the next day seeing that we had just received communion earlier. That was just fine with me, I didn't like going to church anyway.

The following Sunday was to become a day that was to be forever etched into my young mind. Except for my older brother Mike, who was a Cobra Gunship pilot in Vietnam, all eight of us were in attendance that morning. We were later than usual getting to mass that day, so the church was packed. One of the ushers saw our family entering and he gestured for my father to bring us up front for he had saved our family a pew near the alter.

Usually just before Mass started, the church would be filled with the soft hum of people greeting one and other, asking about relatives or recent births and vacations. When the congregation saw all of us enter, the church got dead silent, you could hear a pin drop. All eyes were on us as we were led down to our pew. So many of the faces staring at us had looks of sadness and sympathy, knowing what my father and our family had just been forced to live through. However, I can tell you for sure, there was more than one look of contempt coming from certain eyes that morning. The Terrys were not loved by all. It's sad to say but looking back I feel there was one or two people at mass that were enjoying seeing my father go through so much pain. There are just some people out in the world that are incapable of showing the least amount of empathy. I can only imagine just how hard it must have been for my dad to walk into church that morning, knowing his crazy father and our family were part of everyone's conversations in town. He carried the pain of his mother's tragic demise with him the rest of his life.

My dad told me just before his death in 2003 that he felt so guilty that he failed to get his father committed sooner, avoiding his mother's death. I tried to assure him he played no part in his father's craziness and that he was a great son to both. Dad passed a few days later. Bringing those thoughts with you to your grave was no way to go I thought. Rest in peace dad, I owe you the world.

CHAPTER 16

Typical Sundays

SUNDAYS AT THE Terry household were always very much the same. The entire family would load up and go to 9am Mass down at St. Phillips. After church we would pick up some hard-seeded rolls and crumb buns from the bakery on Main street, then drive home for Sunday breakfast.

Most Sundays when we arrived home from Mass, our uncle Charlie and aunt Cush would be parked out in front of our house waiting for us. You see, Skipper's Pub on Sundays didn't open until 12pm. So, they joined us for breakfast most Sundays, aunt Cush would enjoy my mother's cooking, but uncle Charlie wouldn't eat a thing, instead my dad would line him up with a three-finger glass of Jameson. At five minutes before 12:00 the two of them would hop into their LTD, drive down Seaview, and pull in front of Skippers at 12 on the dot. Their devotion to Northport's watering hole was unmatched.

Even in church, during Mass I could entertain Jean and Paul by making faces or pointing out funny looking parishioners. I carried on with these hijinks knowing full well that if my mother caught wind of my antics, she would rap me in the side of the head. My favorite trick was to take the host wafer the priest gave out at communion and instead of eating it I would lodge it up onto the roof of my mouth and see how long I could keep it up there before it disintegrated. One time I kept the host in my mouth for the ride home and I shocked everyone at the breakfast table when I proudly reached into my mouth and dislodged the soggy host. My mother almost chocked on her bacon and eggs and yelled at me for being sacrilegious. She grabbed me by my ear and took me into the living room and proceeded to put me over her knee and gave me a thorough spanking and sent me off to my room. No Sunday jelly donuts for me, just a sore bottom. To calm things down and to get me out of my mother's hair, my father decided to take me along when he went to see Pop at the hospital. Sunday was the only day my grandfather could have visitors.

CHAPTER 17

Greasing of the Palm

KINGS PARK, AS we locals referred to it, was opened in 1885 and was one of New York State's largest psychiatric hospitals. It sat on 100 acres of rolling hills overlooking the Long Island sound. In the late fifties it was home to 9,000 residents; in 67 there were 5,200 lost souls locked away within it's cold walls.

The ride to the hospital took less than 20 minutes. We drove with the windows down, it was mid-October and the leaves were showing off their bright yellows and reds as if to reminds us that soon our world would be dark and gloomy for the next five months. My mind wandered to thoughts of Halloween and the Rifleman costume my mother was making for me. I was hoping to win best costume this year at Ocean Avenue School. Last year I lost out to a robot costume worn by Michael Milford, an Albert Einstein type of kid who had recently moved to Northport from England. He was the smartest kid in our class and the jerk knew it. That limey was a pain in my ass, and I was not about to lose to him again.

The road leading up to the main group of buildings must have been at least a half mile long. My grandfather was housed on the 10th floor of the infamous building 19, where many of New York's criminally insane lived out their remaining days in cold dank rooms in the basement. Ironically, my grandfather wasn't considered violent, so he was on a much better floor. Dad pulled into a parking spot, turned off the engine and turned to talk to me. He began to explain to me that

Pop had lost his mind and thinks grandma was still alive, so when he asks you how she's doing just tell him she is fine and dandy. Dad bought him a box of candy and told me to refuse any when he asks me if I wanted one.

We entered building 19 through the main doors and stepped into a massive lobby. The two hallways off the lobby were each massive and brightly lit. My father walked up to a security guard sitting behind a desk and said, "Hi Carl, how's the family?"

"Fine Jack," the guard said, then looked at me and said, "You must be John Jr. You coming to visit your Pop today?"

I told the man that I was while my dad signed the visitor's log. Dad then produced a brown paper bag from his back pants pocket and handed it to Carl. I would later learn that the bag contained Carl's favorite brand of whiskey. This was part of the way my dad could get me in to visit Pop.

We walked over to the elevators and hopped into an empty one. I asked dad if I could push the button for floor 10, he said yes but I want to talk to you first and pulled the stop button. He began to explain to me that when we get off the elevator onto pop's floor, we will see a very large man dressed in a white uniform. He was the head orderly, named Ted.

Dad then pulled out a crisp twenty-dollar bill from his wallet and said to me, this is called greasing the palm. He took the bill and folded it several times, so it was not much bigger than a cigarette lighter and pressed it firmly into his palm. He told me that when Ted spots us getting off the elevator, he will walk up and shake my hand and I would slip him the bill.

"I give him 20 dollars every week, this way I know Pop will get nothing but the best treatment," Dad said. (Please keep in mind that in 1967 the minimum wage was only $1.00 an hour). Ted would have done just about anything my father asked. "This is how you grease a palm, it's how the world works," he told me. All I knew was twenty dollars could get me into the Northport movie theatre 40 times.

The elevator stopped at the 10th floor and the doors opened. The first thing that hit me like a ton of bricks was the down right, unpleasant smell that instantly envelopes you like a wet blanket when the elevator doors opened. All I can tell you is that it smelled like all sorts of human body fluids and old people. My dad looked down at me and realized from the look on my face that he should have warned me about the odor. He was probably thinking that maybe it wasn't such a bright idea to bring a 10-year-old to a mental hospital, to visit his grandfather who just got committed for killing his grandmother with a fucking ball peen hammer. Dad leaned down and told me that I would get use to the smell, but I would never forget it. My father and I stepped off the elevator and walked over to the reception desk. My dad told the lady that we were there to see his father, Charles Terry. The lady behind the desk called down to the orderly station and let them know to bring up Mr. Terry for visitors.

The two hallways that ran off from the reception desk were each longer than a football field. I saw several old men like my grandfather walking around aimlessly, dressed in what looked like pajamas. My father said, "Hey, John there's Ted down the hall." I saw a man dressed in all white, not pajamas, but a uniform. He kind of looked like the Good Humor Ice Cream man that drove through our neighborhood in the summer. "Boy this guy Ted sure can walk fast," I said to my father. My father put his finger to his lips to signal me to keep quiet.

This Ted guy was huge but very light and quick on his feet like a hungry tiger. He was on my father like stink on a skunk. Dad and Ted shook hands and I saw the hand-off of the crisp twenty bucks into Ted's hand then into his pants pocket. The exchange happened so smoothly and quickly most people would have never picked up on it. I had just witnessed my first palm greasing. I had no idea at the time that I too would use the old palm grease from time to time when I got older. But instead of mental hospital orderlies, my palm greasing would usually be reserved for snooty restaurant maître D's.

Ted brought us down the hall into the visiting room. The room was about 20′ x 30′ with old time pictures hung on the walls of men on horseback, hunting fox. The room also had a few tables, chairs and two couches. I walked over to the windows and looked out upon the beautiful Long Island Sound, the wind creating large whitecaps before crashing onto the beach. At that moment I felt sorry for my grandfather, knowing in less than an hour I was going to leave this horrible place and return home to my mother and siblings, but poor Pop would never be leaving. We grabbed the couch in the far corner a little set back from the rest of the seating area that afforded us some privacy.

In less than five minutes Ted was back with my grandfather. He was dressed in plain pajamas and had a light grey bathrobe on. He looked very thin and tired, but he managed a smile when our eyes met. For some unknown reason my Pop recognized me. I stood up and gave Pop a hug and handed him a box of mixed chocolates Dad had gotten for him down at Jones's Drug Store. More families and other mental patients began filling up the visitor's room. A lot of the patients had blank expressions on their faces. A few talked in gibberish and there was one old man that constantly made funny sounding noises and was later restrained and taken back to his room. I felt very sad for all of them. Then Pop turned to me and said, "Hey John, how's grandma doing?" I looked at my dad then back at my grandfather and told Pop that grandma was doing well and wishes she could have come to see him. "Maybe next time," he said, then turned and stared out the widow as if he was watching TV. I would go only one more time to visit my grandfather. On the ride back home, my dad told me just how proud he was of me, for handling todays visit as well as I did. Six months later, Charles Scudder Terry died in his sleep, totally oblivious to his killing of his beloved wife Loretta.

CHAPTER 18

Ocean Avenue and Mrs. Huntley

SOME OF MY fondest memories of my time at Ocean Avenue Elementary occurred while I was in the 5th grade and had the best teacher in all of Ocean Avenue, Mrs. Huntley. Mrs. Huntley was in a class of her own. All of us that were lucky enough to have had her as a teacher will go to our graves thinking she was the best. She was warm, kind, understanding and always kept us excited to learn and to be in her class. She was also very protective of her students.

That year in 5th grade we had a very young art teacher named Miss Wolfe, no relation to the 3rd grade teacher that married our principal,

Mr. Welch. Looking back, I think she was straight out of college, in her early twenties and even at my young age I thought her to be quite the looker. Ocean Avenue was probably her first job.

I remember this like it was yesterday. Miss Wolfe came into our room and told us we were just going to have an informal draw what you like day. So, me and some of my best buddies, George Suddell, Tim Smith and Joe Porciello began to draw war scenes of WWII with tanks, jeeps and of course Americans fighting the Germans. All four of us decked out the German tanks with swastikas. When young Miss Wolfe, who unbeknownst to us 5th graders was Jewish; well let's just say she had a meltdown. She grabbed all our drawings and began yelling at us, shouting how disrespectful we all were. It was the worst tongue lashing we had ever received. Mrs. Huntley burst back into the class and grabbed Miss Wolfe by the arm and dragged her out into the hallway. We all could hear Mrs. Huntley tell the art teacher to calm down and collect herself for she was crying. She went on to tell Miss Wolfe that "her" boys had no understanding of what the swastikas meant to Jewish people. "They meant no harm," she said. We didn't see much of Miss Wolfe after our misunderstanding. Me, George, Tim and Joe all thought it was so cool the way Mrs. Huntley had stood up for us. Like I said, she was wonderful.

CHAPTER 19

Pen Pals

ONE OF THE coolest things Mrs. Huntley did was introduce us to pen pals. She formed a relationship with the principal of a New York City elementary school in the middle of China Town. We began exchanging letters with these Chinese immigrants, many of whom were very new to the United States and were just learning English.

That spring of 69, Mrs. Huntley arranged for us to go on a field trip to visit our new pen pals at their school in the city. I still remember the bus ride into the city. For the first half hour our bus driver took us along the country roads of eastern Long Island. Soon the countryside began to give way to the more congested city streets of Nassau County and Queens. Gone were the large yards of Northport. We all found it amazing just how close the homes were located next to each other. I remember thinking that if your best buddy lived next door, all you had to do was to open your bedroom windows and talk.

We crossed over the Triborough bridge and looked with amazement at the massive city skyline before us, the Big Apple in all its grandeur. None of us 5th graders knew at the time but, within 15 years about a third of the kids in my class would be commuting each day in and out of New York on the infamous Long Island Railroad. My fellow classmates and I were amazed with the city streets with all the new sights, sounds and smells. Our driver parked the bus a block away from our pen pal's school. We walked past some strange looking stores. One such store looked like a Chinese version of a local deli but instead of different types of meat hanging in the front window, this store proudly showcased cooked ducks, hanging from their necks with their heads still on. This sight, at least for the boys, made the long bus ride from Northport well worth it.

I remember meeting my pen pal and how proud all the kids were of their school. Mind you, it was in good condition, but it was everything Ocean Avenue was not. It was small and cramped with a tiny blacktop playground which our pen pals' thought was great. After touring their classrooms and school we were treated to what was to be for most of us, our first truly authentic Chinese lunch at a local restaurant. It was my first introduction to wonton soup. I loved every spoonful of the flavorful broth and the delicate, meat-filled wontons. To this day it is still one of my all-time favorite soups.

A few weeks later our Chinese pen pals took a field trip out to Northport. For most of the kids it was their first time being more than a few blocks away from their homes, let alone 50 miles away into the suburbs of north shore of Long island. I still remember looks on their faces as they walked off the bus. They looked like they had just been to the moon. Our pen pals were amazed at the size of our massive grass playground. After having lunch, the real excitement started.

Mrs. Huntley arranged for all of us to ride down town to the park and docks to go fishing and to give our pen pals rides in motor boats. Several fathers with boats volunteered to take the city kids on rides. My pen pal had never gone fishing before. The sand worms we used for bait, with their hocked pincers that they kept hidden in their mouths really scared my pen pal. He made it quite clear to me through his broken English that he wanted me to worm the fishing hook. It wasn't long after dropping the line into Northport harbor that my pen pal began to scream in excitement. He was flabbergasted at hooking a Sea Robin. Not a prized fish by any means but to my pen pal from the city it was like he had just pulled in Moby Dick. I'm willing to guess that every one of those city kids still remember their first true adventure in their new country. Northport and its surrounding harbor have a way of getting into your blood, never allowing you to escape its allure. I guess that's what I love most of all.

CHAPTER 20

6th Grade

THE FOLLOWING YEAR I entered the 6th grade. We were the first group of kids to have class rooms in the newly constructed wing at Ocean Avenue. The February before a fire broke out in the 30-year-old wing that contained 12 classrooms.

My teacher was a man named Mr. Eddy. Mr. Eddy came out of retirement for some unknown reason and took a job as our new 6th grade teacher. He was old school. Certainly not as nice as Mrs. Huntley and he and I locked horns right from the get-go. He was very demanding of me and it seemed to me that Mr. Eddy didn't really care for me that much.

I remember one time in class I said to Mr. Eddy that I have been hearing all this talk on the news about abortion. What is abortion I asked? Well, Mr. Eddy's face got beet red and he snapped at me that abortion was not a topic of conversation in his classroom, I should go home and ask my parents to explain it to you. Of course, he was right, but did he really have to have a bird over it.

As the school year progressed things got better between me and Mr. Eddy. He was calmer and more relaxed, and I think I was starting to mature and grow up. Just before the end of school the entire 6th grade was called down to the gym for a special announcement.

There were five classes of sixth graders at Ocean Avenue and all of us sat on the gym floor filled with excitement as to what the special announcement was going to be. Mr. Welch, our school Principal, stood up and began to tell all of us that in two weeks anyone who can get their parents permission will be going on an over night field trip to a farm up in Pauling, New York. The gym exploded with shouts of excitement, we were going on an overnight adventure.

Most of my fellow classmates were able to get their parent's permission to go on our over night field trip. The dozen or so kids that were not allowed to go for one reason or another all had to attend Mr. Eddy's class the two days we lucky kids were gone. We all felt sorry for them being stuck behind.

Two weeks later we all packed into busses for the 100-mile trip up the Hudson River Valley and within three hours we pulled into the long country driveway that brought us to a huge red barn that had been converted into bunk houses, a large kitchen and dining hall. There was another much smaller building that looked more like a house a little set back from the main building.

This smaller building had eight beds in it and as fate would have it me, Jeremy Brinsmead and George Suddell and five other boys were selected to sleep, unattended mind you, away from the main building. I still wonder why the teachers decided to put we three Amigos together out in that building unchaperoned? Me, George and Jeremy weren't bad kids, but we were well known boys that liked to be daring and were filled with all sorts of mischief. We were also three of the oldest boys at Ocean Avenue, seeing that all three of us had been held back a grade. Maybe that's why the teachers paired us up with the five other boys that were all very shy and socially insecure. In any event, trouble was soon to follow. How could it not?

The property had to be a couple hundred acers, bordered by a huge hill, lush with thick green grass and thousands of dandelions. We all could run freely up and down the hill and anywhere else on the farm.

At the bottom of the hill was a large pond that was packed with more frogs than any of us had ever seen. There was a partially submerged tree in the middle of the pond and several of its branches were above the waterline. To our delight, dozens of big fat frogs sun bathed on these branches and weren't fazed one bit that 15 or so 6th grade boys began throwing rocks at them. What a blast we had, trying to hit the frogs. We began to hit a few frogs and none of us were bothered when they simply floated, lifeless in the water.

Our frog hunting ended abruptly when my buddy, Tom Michaels, who later in life was to become a big-time college pitcher, threw a side arm that hit the grand pappy of all frogs' square in the head. The poor frog exploded on impact. Several of the girls that had been watching screamed hysterically at Tom's knock-out. Mr. Marshall ran over to us and put a stop to our tomfoolery.

Pauling Farm wasn't all fun and games, we did do some learning. When the entire group was assembled in the dining hall, we watched a movie about being good stewards to our environment. Keep in mind this was the late sixties and the lower Hudson and East rivers were a stinking cesspool. The forerunner of todays environmental movement was just starting to gain attraction. After the movie a lot of us helped in the large kitchen and made baked chicken for dinner. Then the real fun began.

When it was time for all of us to hit the hey for the night, the main group of kids went upstairs to the dormitories and we lucky eight were led out to our private sleeping quarters by our likable gym teacher, Mr. Marshall. Man did he read us the riot act. He looked me, George and Jeremy square in the eyes and warned us what would happen if he had to come back here in the middle of the night. There would be hell to pay he told us. After his little speech, Mr. Marshall hurried back to the main building and probably began to party with the other teachers while we slept, or so they thought.

Lights out was at 9pm. We began our fun right after. All eight of us laid out in a circle on the floor and dumped out our snacks our mothers had packed for us and shared everything. The box of Drake's Funny Bones my mother sent with me were a big hit. We laid there for hours talking late into the night. I had a flashlight and told a ghost story I heard from my older sister and one of the other boys, who will remain unnamed, began to cry like a baby.

George Suddell, who hung out with older guys in his neighborhood and thought he was now an expert about girls, began to tell us what we can expect to happen when we start dating girls in high school. Please bear in mind that although I had a brother, he was 13 years older and fighting in the jungles of Vietnam. I was basically raised with three older sisters and my father hadn't yet given me the "birds and bees" talk. George thought he was so cool, but I know he didn't understand everything he was telling us. All I knew was that none of my sisters did those kinds of things, well maybe my sister Theresa did, mom said she had turned into a hippie child and had gotten uncontrollable.

After our story telling session, we broke off into 2 teams and had the best pillow fights a young guy could have asked for. Jeremy was by far the strongest of us all. When Jeremy moved to Northport 4 years earlier from England, due to Great Brittan's school system lagging our US school system in their teaching, Jeremy was held back two years to allow him to catch up. He was old enough to be in 8th grade and was quite a bit stronger. His pillow strikes didn't exactly tickle. He landed a blow to one of the shy boys right in the face and made his nose to bleed. The boy began to cry and ran out of the house yelling he was going to get Mr. Marshall. We all panicked with thoughts of mad man Marshall returning with the cry baby at 2 in the morning. Jeremy just ran and caught up to our roommate just before he walked into the main building and threw him over his shoulder and ran back to our cabin kicking and screaming the entire way. We calmed him down, cleaned up his bloody nose and told him if he spilled the beans on us, we were going to tell all the kids he peed his bed. That shut him right up.

The next morning, we all got up and had a good laugh over what had happened and the fantastic night we all had. Even the nose bleeder was laughing. Looking back, I think those five shy boys loved every minute of our craziness and camaraderie. It was probably the first time most of them really felt like they belonged to a group, a pack and it was fun to go wild from time to time. Boys being boys.

CHAPTER **21**

Northport Junior High

MY FIRST TWO years of Junior High weren't exactly what I would call enjoyable. Seventh and eighth grade can be very awkward for a lot of kids and I was no exception. My first two years of junior high I stilled carried what our family physician, Dr. Saltz called baby fat. Let's face it, I was 5'7" and chubby. I was a well-liked kid by most, outgoing and was good at playing baseball and football and had many friends. But I was still trying to figure out just where I stood in the social pecking order of junior high school.

Junior high is when I stopped singing in a chorus. All throughout elementary school I sang in the school chorus and loved every minute of it. In 6th grade I was chosen by Mrs. Baldwin to sing a solo at the schools Christmas concert. It was quite an honor to be chosen.

When I hit junior high it was a different story. I joined the junior high chorus in 7th grade but when 8th grade came around I approached our music teacher, Mr. Butts and told him I wouldn't be singing in the chorus anymore. He was very surprised with my decision and asked me why I no longer wanted to sing? I told him I just lost interest in singing. That was a big fat lie, I loved singing. The problem was there were no real cool or popular kids in chorus, so I thought, and my friends made fun of me for being in the chorus. I folded and walked away from something I really enjoyed.

Looking back, I was such a fool to have caved in to peer pressure. I didn't cave two years before when my friends tried to get me to smoke cigarettes, there was no way I was going to smoke that crap. But chorus, that was a different story. There were no cool kids in chorus. Mr. Butts even called my parents and told them I was making a mistake. He went on to tell them that I hat perfect pitch and it was a gift not to be squandered. I stuck to my guns and I have never sung in a chorus again. A mistake I regret to this day.

My friends in junior high consisted of mostly the same guys I had gone to school with at Ocean Avenue. As far as the opposite sex went, I knew all the girls in my class and was friendly with them all, especially the pretty ones. Junior high school is really the time most boys notice and seek out the girls that catch their eye and I was no exception. I was however, a bit on the plump side in 7th and 8th grade and I am afraid my attraction was one sided. My best friend, George Suddell, by 8th grade already had girlfriends where I was merely looked upon as nice John Terry. But that was all soon to change.

CHAPTER 22

My First Kiss

THE SUMMER OF 1972 was transformative for me both physically and mentally. I don't know what happened, but I grew to 5'10" and I was 170 pounds and no longer chubby. I was lean, much stronger thanks to lifting weights all summer and I became much faster. I could feel the change and knew things were going to be different for me when I went back to Northport Junior High as a 9th grader. I was anxious to get to know girls on a new level as well and I didn't have to wait too long for my first opportunity.

A couple of weeks before school started a bunch of my friends and I were hanging out in the basement of Robby Latino's parents' house. His parents were out for the night and we had gotten our hands on a bunch of beer. We were listing to music, drinking, having a good old time when the doorbell rang. It was several of the girls we knew from school. Beers were passed all around, the Allman Brothers' *Eat a Peach* album was being played and before I knew it, one of the girls I had known most of my entire young life, took me by the hand and led me into Mr. Latino's small office. She pushed me down onto the office chair, got on top of me a proceeded to give me my first long, life changing kiss. We stopped our kissing for a moment, just long enough for my friend to look me in the eyes as if she was having trouble recognizing me and said, "You know, I don't remember you ever looking like you do now John, what happened?" I smiled and replied "it must be the salt air", then went right back to our make out session. She told me I was a good kisser. There was no way I was going to admit to her then and there that this was my first. You never forget your first kiss. After that night I was hooked, I loved girls and couldn't wait for the start of the new school year.

CHAPTER 23

9th Grade, My Last Year in Northport

I COULD HARDLY finish the nice breakfast of pancakes and bacon my mother had cooked for us. I didn't get much sleep and was up extra early, and beyond anxious to get to school. I told my younger sister Jean who was entering the 7th grade to hurry up or else she would be walking to school by herself. We cut through the Berglund's back yard and started our mile long walk to junior high. Jean was just as excited as I was to start a new year in a new school, although she and her friends would be on the bottom of the school totem pole. She didn't care, she knew I wouldn't let anyone give her a hard time.

I entered my 9th grade homeroom and greeted many of the kids I already knew. When our homeroom teacher told us to settle down and be seated, I looked across the room to a blonde girl I had never seen before. She had to be new to Northport. She turned and smiled at me.

There have been a handful of girls and women in my life that at the first-time laying eyes upon them, have caused my heart to skip a beat due to their sheer beauty. This is exactly what happened to me when I first laid eyes on Sue Thomas. To me she was a goddess. She had beautiful long blonde hair, piercing brown eyes and was curvy in all the right places, much more so than most of the other girls in our class. What can I tell you, I was infatuated? Our encounter would have to wait many months for me to work up my nerve to approach her.

Up to this point, 9th grade was the best part of my life. As we got older, my close bonds with my guy friends only grew stronger. We all had ten-speed bikes and rode them from up at Carvel all the way down to Asharoken, Waterside Park and Crab Meadow Beach. We spent a lot of time hanging down town in the village, meeting up with girls in the park, going to the movies and having parties in the woods like most kids. Probably the single most stupid and danger-ous decision my friends and I ever made as young teenagers was to attempt to walk across the frozen, ice covered Northport harbor in early January of 1973. That winter was bitterly cold and for the first time in our young lives the harbor had frozen over. We decided one night we were going to walk across the ice to check out the Vanderbilt Museum. The six of us got about 200 feet across when we all stopped and looked at each other with genuine fear. The ice was moving with the waves below, causing us to be lifted with each passing wave. Without saying a word, we all turned and slowly began our walk back to the dock.

All at once, two Northport police cars hit us with their search lights. We froze in place and heard the cops yell at us over their bullhorn, "you crazy kids, stay where you are, some firemen are com-ing out to get you". Two Northport Firemen pushed an aluminum row boat out to us and had us get in and brought us back to the town docks. Waiting for us were several pissed off cops and several Firemen. They yelled at us big time and rightly so. We were taken to the police station and had to call our parents to come and get us. We all were in hot water for quite some time. God was surely looking out for us that night, none of us fell through the rolling harbor ice. Stupid teenage boys, thinking there're invincible.

I was really having the time of my life when my father knocked the wind out of me, and announced at dinner one night just before Christmas, that we were going to be moving to Andover, MA once school got out. Andover was the town my father's only sister; my aunt Mary had moved to in the early sixties. We had visited Andover many times and I liked going to visit my cousins but my God, it wasn't Northport. We Terrys have been in Northport for 200 years I proclaimed, why did we have to move. I put the thought of moving away from Northport out of my mind, convinced I had time to talk the old man out of the idea and went on with life.

I'm not proud to admit it, but the year of 9th grade was the year my friends and I became drinkers. Every chance we got on a Friday or Saturday night had us trying to get our hands on some booze. We would either get an older sibling to buy for us or from time to time, George Suddell, the biggest of our pack could buy at the German deli down at Hills grocery store plaza. The old kraut that owned the deli either thought George was 18 or really didn't give a dam as long George had money in hand. And of course, George thought he was so stinking cool being the only one out of our gang able to fool the Kiser, but he was still my best friend. By the time my birthday came around the end of April when I turned 16 I was resigned to the fact we were moving to Andover.

The thought of moving away from Northport up to the Boston area turned my stomach. At 16 I thought my life was soon coming to an end. Little did I know that I was going to learn to love Andover and its people, become part of a two-time back to back, division one, Massachusetts state champion football team and make new and strong to this day, lifelong friendships.

The spring of 1973 after my birthday things seemed to have flown by. Before I knew it, it was early June and school was just two short weeks from ending. My parents planned for us to move the day after school got out. I had only two weeks and I still hadn't got the courage to tell Sue Thomas just how much I liked her. Soon, I'll do it soon, I told myself.

The day before school got out some of us were over at Rob Latinos house. We had come up with the plan to make home-made smoke bombs and light them off at school the next day, the last day of junior high. We ran up to the Big Apple Plaza and next to Eddy's Pizza was a small drug store. Back in 1973 you could buy over the counter salt-peter, one of the ingredients of gunpowder. Back at Rob's house we took sugar, melted it down, added the saltpeter and poured the thick goo into two empty OJ cans. When the saltpeter and sugar began to get hard, we took fusses from firecrackers and placed them into our smoke bombs. We were all set. We had no idea the panic we were going to unleash at school.

My heart pounded the entire walk to school. It was a day with many mixed emotions. I was so sad and depressed over the fact that I was to move away in less than 24 hours, the only home I had ever known. But I was also very excited about seeing how effective our smoke bombs were going to be. And the icing on the cake was that one of the girls I was friendly with for the past eight years was having an end-of-school party at her house tonight. Our friend Phil and his band were going to be playing there. Best of all, Sue Thomas told me she wouldn't miss the party and the chance to say good-bye to me. I had a hard time containing myself.

There were a lot of kids mulling around the back of the school, waiting for the entrance bell. There was so much excitement in the air at the prospect of starting summer vacation you could cut it with a knife. If they only knew their last day of school was going to come to a quick and smoky end way before our scheduled release of 11:00.

We pyros huddled up for one last review of the plans. Two of my buddies, who will remain unnamed were to place the two smoke bombs in lockers, one down in the newer one-story addition and the other smoker was to be placed in the 2nd floor front stairwell. They were to light cigarettes and shove the fuses into the smokes and run to homeroom.

About ten minutes later when everyone was settled down to what was to be an enjoyable short last day of school, our homemade smoke bombs went off like clockwork. So much smoke poured out of them you would have thought it was the end of days, Armageddon. Suddenly the fire alarm sounded off and we were all led outside. The entire fire department along with four Northport Police cars came screeching onto school property. The principal and the fire and police were pissed off big time. A few of us including me were questioned but we all denied, denied, denied. What could they do? They had no proof. No cell phone cameras in 1973, thank God. And what could they do to me? I was moving to Boston in the morning. School was let out without any of us going back in, too much smoke. It was 9:45. What a caper we had just pulled off. If it happened today, Homeland Security and the FBI would be on the spot looking to pin it on someone.

Later that day just before dinner, I was upstairs in the bathroom putting on my stepping-out shirt when I heard my father pull into the driveway. He was returning home with some pizzas from Salvatore's. It was to be my last Salvatore's pizza for quite some time. I had learned a few years back while visiting my cousins in Andover that most pizza shops in the Boston area were owned and operated by Greek people. Nothing against the Greeks mind you, they made great shish kabob, but their pizza sucked compared to good, Italian made, long Island Pizza.

After dinner my friends and I met in the woods up at Ocean Avenue school to drink and get a little oiled-up before making it down the road to Carolyn's house for the party. When we got there Phil's band had just begun to play some tunes and a lot of the kids were coming up to me, telling me good luck and goodbye. I looked across the backyard and Sue and I locked eyes and headed toward each other. We went inside and sat on the basement steps, holding hands and listening to music. Sue told me she wished I had made a move way before tonight. What can I tell you, I was young and not too experienced with the ladies? Not to mention the fact Sue's beauty overpowered any confidence I may have had, and I was too afraid of rejection. It turned out to be a wonderful night. The party was a blast, I was with all my closet friends and I was I finally having my make out session with Sue Thomas. What a sendoff. 45 years later and I still remember every detail of my last night in Northport.

The next morning was tough to deal with. Two of my buddies, George Suddell and Tom Michaels came over to see me off. On June 23rd, 1973 we pulled away from our beautiful home on Seaview Avenue for the long ride up to Andover and my soon to be new life away from Northport. Like I have said before, Northport has a way of grabbing you by the heart and never letting you go. I will always miss you, sweet lady.

CHAPTER **24**

Andover

I CAN'T BEGIN to tell you just how depressing that 250-mile drive up to Andover Massachusetts was. With no warning, I felt all my emotions tie a knot in the pit of my stomach, as my dad crossed over the Throgs Neck and I gazed out the window to the New York City skyline. I was so looking forward to getting to know the City intimately when I got a little older. It looks like now I'll be cutting my teeth on the City streets of Bean Town.

My parents, as always, smoked the entire way cracking the windows ever so slightly. There was so much smoke in the interior of our car a person could cure a Sothern ham by the time we reached New England. Secondhand smoke, what the hell was that? In 73, people still lit-up just about anywhere, in planes, trains and automobiles and in the front seat of my old man's Caddie.

What was I going to do? My dad bought a house several miles from the center of down town Andover. I had grown up in Northport being able to get to the town village in five short minutes. I knew everyone and they all knew me. My young adult life was just starting to take off back in Northport. I hung out with the same kids since third grade.. Who was I going to meet and become friends with? I hated my life. I didn't want to be in fucking Andover.

We pulled into our new driveway around 3:00 that day. Me, Jean and Paul almost burst out in tears. Our new home was a modern, small split level. We had left a six bedroom, 100-year-old Victorian for this modern cube of a house. I thought it was all a bad dream. The only saving grace was my dad had promised us he would put in a built-in pool. Three weeks later it was in the ground. After checking out the inside of our new home we headed down to Andover village to have dinner at our aunt and uncle's house. My three cousins tried to assure me that I would quickly make new friends once high school and football started. I told them I didn't want anything to do with lousy Andover. Unbeknownst to me at the time, tomorrow was going to present some interesting new distractions.

The next morning, my first real day in our new town began like most. My mother made me breakfast and told me after eating I was to go out and start unloading the cars. Stepping out from our air-conditioned new home I was hit with a thick wave of heat. I thought for sure it was going to be a littler cooler up in New England compared to Long Island. Man was I wrong. At least back in Northport we had the constant, blowing wind coming off the sound to help cool us off on hot humid days. Not here in Andover, no breeze what so ever.

I started thinking about what my friends back in Northport would be doing today? The beach probably, a whole bunch of them would be spending most of the day down at Crab Meadow and maybe they would hit the movies later that night or a party in the woods. Me, I was stuck unloading boxes in my new lame ass town.

I was feeling sorry for myself, reaching way into the trunk of my father's car and grabbing a box when I heard a voice behind me. "Hey new kid." I slowly turned around and standing there in my driveway was a girl about my age, a very pretty girl. She had long brown hair, was well tanned, wearing short shorts and a very revealing halter top. She looked me up and down, smiled and said, "Hey new kid, you want to go run off into the woods and smoke some grass?" I stood there speechless for five seconds looking at this new beauty before me. I then looked to the heavens and said, "Northport, what's Northport?" My new adventures in Andover had just begun.

CPSIA information can be obtained
at www.ICGtesting.com
Printed in the USA
BVHW081029231119
564634BV00001B/184/P

9 781977 219619